Loving

MW00344881

Education

Burnout runs rampant in education, particularly in the field of special education, and has only increased with the rise of virtual and remote learning. This book compiles 50 evidence-based strategies and practices to help special educators enjoy their work for the long haul. You'll discover new ways to work with families, manage your classroom, teach in culturally responsive ways, and prioritize self-care. Each chapter includes an opening vignette, key themes supported by research, and five reproducible tools to put into immediate practice. With strategies and tools to ensure classroom fun and satisfaction, this book reminds special education teachers of the life-changing work they do every day and is essential for teachers of any level.

Rachel R. Jorgensen is a special educator, college professor, and educational writer with a special interest in empowering learners with special needs. She has spent nearly 20 years in the special education classroom and continues to enjoy her daily work with her students.

Loving Your Job in Special Education

50 Tips and Tools

Rachel R. Jorgensen

Routledge
Taylor & Francis Group

NEW YORK AND LONDON

Cover image: © Getty Images

First published 2023
by Routledge
605 Third Avenue, New York, NY 10158

and by Routledge
4 Park Square, Milton Park, Abingdon, Oxon, OX14 4RN

Routledge is an imprint of the Taylor & Francis Group, an informa business

Library of Congress Cataloging-in-Publication Data
Names: Jorgensen, Rachel R, author.
Title: Loving your job in special education : 50 tips and tools / Rachel R Jorgensen.
Description: First Edition. | New York : Routledge, 2023. | Series: Eye On Education Books | Includes bibliographical references.
Identifiers: LCCN 2022021155 (print) | LCCN 2022021156 (ebook) | ISBN 9781032345130 (Hardback) | ISBN 9781032342689 (Paperback) | ISBN 9781003322528 (eBook)
Subjects: LCSH: Special education teachers—Job stress. | Burn out (Psychology)—Prevention. | Teacher turnover—Prevention. | Stress management. | Special education—Psychological aspects.
Classification: LCC LB2840.2 .J676 2023 (print) | LCC LB2840.2 (ebook) | DDC 371.9/043—dc23/eng/20220810
LC record available at https://lccn.loc.gov/2022021155
LC ebook record available at https://lccn.loc.gov/2022021156

ISBN: 978-1-032-34513-0 (hbk)
ISBN: 978-1-032-34268-9 (pbk)
ISBN: 978-1-003-32252-8 (ebk)

DOI: 10.4324/9781003322528

Typeset in Palatino
by Apex CoVantage, LLC

Access the Support Material: www.routledge.com/9781032342689

To all the amazing educators who have helped to shape who I am both as a special education teacher and a person. You know who you are!

To Bennett and Samri, who remind me to live with gratitude, purpose, and love every day. You amaze me, and you are my whole heart. Love, Mom.

Contents

Introduction

I'm so glad this book is in your hands. I hope it brings you joy, energy, and some useful tips to help you enjoy your adventure as a special education teacher. Any special education teacher can feel like a baby chick on the freeway at times. Be proud of yourself for rising to the challenge! Keep a light heart and don't stop smiling as you reflect on the completely open and honest perspective offered in this book. After years and years in the special education classroom, I have learned so

> This book is designed to help you avoid common pitfalls in order to thrive and fall in love with your job in special education.

much through a multitude of mishaps, errors, and mistakes. This book includes a collection of the lessons I have learned, as well as stories of other special education teachers who have navigated the exciting and sometimes murky waters of the special education world. This book is designed to help you avoid common pitfalls in order to thrive and fall in love with your job in special education. I also hope that you stay in love with your special education job forever (or at least until retirement, perhaps?) Happy reading!

DOI: 10.4324/9781003322528-1

Why Did I Write This Book?

The world of education is awash in teacher burnout. For those of us in special education, this problem is especially dire. Over the years, I have seen so many colleagues disheartened when they don't see their hard work paying off with their students. They get the sense that they are shoveling diamonds into a black hole. Many talented teachers fall into frustration and cynicism over the years as they struggle to see the fruits of their labors. Add the pressures of paperwork, parents, and principals, and you have a recipe for stress. What is a special educator to do? Well, first, pause to take pride in the fact that you chose this worthy profession in the first place, or it chose you. Second, open your mind as you read this book and try the strategies listed. Here you will find a thoughtful and strategic pathway to help you sustain yourself in special education for the long haul. Your students will thrive when you do!

Special education is infinitely important for students and is notoriously understaffed. Over the last three decades, schools across the globe have seen a shortage of qualified special education teachers. A high turnover rate among special education teachers, which has remained relatively stable at around 25% over the past 20 years, contributes to this shortage (IRIS Center, 2022). There is also a vast and ongoing need for new special education teachers to join the profession. Special education teacher burnout harms students. According to the Bureau of Labor and Statistics, the demand for special education teachers is expected to grow by 8% by 2026, which means that school districts are more than eager to fill expected vacancies (Bureau of Labor and Statistics, 2021).

I have been a special education teacher for nearly two decades, and I have learned much along the way. Here's the thing: I still love my work with students in special education every single day. Truly! I don't dread Monday morning, and I don't lose sleep on Sunday night. My heart is happy to bring my energy and love to my practice. How? Through the tools you will find in this book. As an instructor in a graduate program for special education teachers, I have discovered that burnout runs rampant among my college students who are largely paraprofessionals and special educators, even those who have been in the role for only a year or two! Thus, my mission is to help special educators thrive in their work and overcome stressors so that they may benefit students, families, and the whole wide world. We have the unique chance to make a difference, so let's dig in and discover how to protect ourselves from the negativity which constantly encroaches in our field.

What Will You Find in this Book?

This book includes a collection of lessons learned by special educators during their time in the classroom. These teachers have navigated the exciting and sometimes murky waters of the special education world. Each chapter includes practical strategies to help you reflect on your role and take good care of yourself along the way. Please note that all identifying information, such as names, locations, etc. have been changed to uphold the privacy of the individuals described. Also, please note that in the author's view, a 'special educator' may be anyone who works with students with disabilities, including psychologists, counselors, service providers, paraprofessionals, educational assistants, and interventionists. All may benefit from the tools and approaches in this book.

> This book is all about LOVE. For yourself, for your students, and for your profession.

This book is all about LOVE. For yourself, for your students, and for your profession. The content, resources, and strategies are designed to help you maintain your sense of motivation, gratitude, and purpose every day. Teaching has never been more difficult for all educators, everywhere, and special educators are taxed to the max. It breaks my heart every time I encounter a graduate school student who arrives in my class completely burned out on the profession, and they have only just begun.

This book is 100% focused on the idea that you can STAY IN LOVE with special education through the use of the right mindset and approaches. That love will translate to students and help them sustain themselves at school. Just as times are tough for teachers, times are just as tough for students. Throw on some challenges related to special educational needs, and you have a recipe for a pretty exhausted and disheartened kid. Approach your work with enthusiasm, joy, and love, and you can change things for the better for students who need it most.

So let's begin.

References

Bureau of Labor and Statistics. (2021). Occupational outlook handbook: Special education teachers. *U.S. Bureau of Labor and Statistics.* www.bls.gov/ooh/education-training-and-library/special-education-teachers.htm#tab-6.

IRIS Center. (2022). Teacher retention and turnover. *Vanderbilt University.* https://iris.peabody.vanderbilt.edu/module/tchr-ret/cresource/q1/p01/

1

Lasting Rewards

'Hey, Ms. James!' Shannon James, a middle school special education teacher, turns in the produce aisle of the grocery stores after hearing her name. She sees one of the store employees, a man in his mid-20s, wearing a green polo shirt and smiling. His name tag reads Juan.

'Juan Velenco?' she asks.

'That's me!'

Juan had been one of Shannon's students ten years ago. When he'd arrived at her middle school, it was the fifteenth school he had attended, and he had gaps in almost every content area. Along with her team, she worked diligently to identify his needs and try to meet them. She found that his language skills were the underlying cause of his difficulties with reading, writing, behavior, and emotional regulation. Through the concerted efforts of the speech/language pathologist, some amazing general education teachers, dedicated special education teachers, and yes, even a kindly custodian who took Juan under his wing, she saw some major gains with Juan over his seventh-grade year. And then almost as suddenly as he'd arrived, his family moved away.

*'Juan! W*ow*! I haven't seen you in years! How are you?' she exclaimed.*

'Well, I got a job, and I love it. I'm helping my mom pay the bills. She bought a house. I like this job. Also, I really like cats. Do you have a cat, Ms. James?'

Yes, this was the same Juan she knew years ago.

DOI: 10.4324/9781003322528-2

'Nope, I have a little dog,' Shannon answered. 'And by the way, you don't have to call me Ms. James. You must be, like, 20 years old by now. Please, call me Shannon.'

'I'm 23 years old, and my birthday is in five months and seven days,' Juan replied quickly with excited anticipation in his voice.

'Well, happy birthday in five months and seven days,' she replied. They continued their chat over a bin of fruit, and Juan's manager even strolled over to say hello. After learning that Ms. Shannon had been Juan's teacher, the manager shared that Juan was one of his most consistent employees, always on time, always willing to work hard.

After that, Shannon saw Juan all the time when she was picking up her groceries. She saw a human being who had found a peaceful life. She saw a student who had been through a tumult of struggle throughout his years growing up but who had made it through and could hold down a job. She recalled her frustration when Juan moved away. He had been making so much progress, and she feared he wouldn't retain anything. She'd wondered what would become of him.

Crossing paths with 23-year-old Juan helped her realize something that has sustained countless special education teachers: her time with students matters, even if she doesn't realize it at the time.

Every single day, you are planting seeds with our students. Every time you cultivate a new academic ability, model a social or emotional skill, or even offer a relational investment through empathy, a seed may be planted. Sometimes it seems as if these seeds are falling among the rocks, and they will never grow. Sometimes it seems like a drought has descended, and they will dry up and die. The most happy and content special education teachers believe that most of the time, those seeds flourish into something helpful and meaningful to the student. The truth is, you most often don't get to see the seeds you have sown develop into fully sprouted plants, but rest assured, they are out there somewhere growing and thriving and basking in the sunshine. Just as Ms. James had no idea about Juan's success until a chance encounter, you may not see the fruition of their labors until much further down the road. With this understanding, you can sustain yourself best when you tend to your sense of hope in your students and in your own potential impact. This is what special education is all about: hope. Teaching a skill is an act of hope that the student will learn and grow. Writing an Individual Education Plan (IEP) is an act of hope that the content will work to make school a better experience for the student. Even showing up each morning is an act of hope that you will engage with students in a way that helps them grow.

> You can choose each day to grow more cynical or more hopeful. You can let the difficulties drag you down, or you can look forward to the possibilities which exist for your students.

You can choose each day to grow more cynical or more hopeful. You can let the difficulties drag you down, or you can look forward to the possibilities which exist for your students. It helps to remember that teachers don't always get to see the successes firsthand, and that's just part of the deal. Somewhere out there, a seed you lovingly planted might just be the mightiest oak in the forest. Rest assured that by showing up and never giving up, YOU ARE MAKING A DIFFERENCE. I promise. How can you up the chances that you will have a lasting positive impact? Through the strategies and approaches listed in this chapter. This chapter invites you to explore questions to help you realize lasting rewards with your students, such as the following:

◆ How can we have FUN with our students to help turn school into a positive experience for them?
◆ How might we create productive learning spaces in special education which are also enjoyable for students?
◆ What are some approaches we can use to help students engage more, learn more, and like school more?
◆ How can we invite students to replace their negative narratives on school and their own abilities with a NEW and BETTER story?
◆ How might we serve as purveyors of hope to sustain our students and subsequently ourselves?
◆ What are some strategies we can use to identify and capitalize on student strengths?

Find Fun Every Day

'I hate this school.'
    'That teacher doesn't like me.'

'As soon as I'm old enough, I'm dropping out anyway.'

Over my years in special education, I cannot count how many times I have heard these heartbreaking statements from students. By the time students reach placement in special education, most students have probably had some intensely difficult experiences at school. To qualify for services, schools must officially prove that things aren't working for the student as they are. Somewhere along the line, students have realized that things just aren't working for them the way they seem to work for other students. This is painful and even traumatic for so many students. Compounding this with the fact that peers tend to perceive when someone is different and can be quite cruel, you have a recipe for a true disaster in the lives of students in need of special education services. Once they qualify, students may experience even further difficulty as they wrestle with the stigma surrounding the concept of disability and the ableism which is alive and well in our schools and society. This all sounds quite bleak indeed.

> Here is the GREAT news: special education can become a space of healing, recovery, and FUN for students!

Here is the GREAT news: special education can become a space of healing, recovery, and FUN for students! As special education teachers, we have the unique opportunity to completely shift the narrative from one of pain and struggle to one of hope and success. Students need to experience the school world as a space that connects to their values, needs, and interests. One of the most universal among these needs is the desire for FUN. People, especially those of the younger variety, are hardwired to desire fun. According to Dr. William Glasser, human beings are genetically wired to meet certain needs, including fun or enjoyment, and this is universal across cultures (Wubbolding, 2015).

How might you begin to create a fun environment in your learning spaces? It starts with empathy. Pause to take an honest look at what you are doing and put yourself in your students' shoes. Forty-minute lectures? Not fun. Worksheet packets? Not fun. Long lists of detailed rules? Not fun. Reading assignments from humongous textbooks with tiny print which feel like heavy bricks in a student's backpack? Yikes. No fun at all. Infuse your practice with innovation and creativity so that you can deliver your content in a way that is fun and engaging to the greatest extent possible. It's okay to ditch the traditional approaches which drag us all down. Fearlessly try new things and you will be surprised by the positive outcomes for your students!

I recommend that you think back to yourself as a child when thinking about bringing fun to your practice, imagining yourself when they were young. Perhaps you were high energy, chatty, partial to a good time, rambunctious, and perhaps not the greatest listener? Yes, I am definitely describing myself circa third grade. Thinking about my earliest memories of school, I remember captivity in a desk chair with a hard and uncomfortable seat. I remember chewing on my pencil and tearing up little pieces of paper to entertain myself. I remember frequent trips to get a drink or hang out in the bathroom to assuage my excessive energy and boredom. I remember frustrated teachers who didn't know what to do with my energy and my busy brain. As time progressed, I learned to 'play the game' at school in order to keep myself out of trouble and achieve decent grades. For so many students, the ability to play the game is not within their skill set, and they endure discomfort with who they are.

We must learn to accept our students' basic need for fun and bring this into their school experiences. They just weren't built to sit and listen, and this isn't how they learn. The more teachers talk, the less they hear. So what's the answer? To create interactive, meaningful, interesting learning experiences in which students have the chance to explore content on their own as we guide them along the way. Table 1.1 offers practical ideas to bring fun into learning experiences for students at any age level and with any types of special needs.

One of the best ways to create a fun and productive space for students is to learn as much as we can about what truly matters to them. What is important to them outside of school? What drives them and brings them joy? Offer students opportunities to express their preferences and interests and then incorporate this in daily classroom activities. Do students enjoy free time on their phones? Incorporate scheduled 'technology breaks' at manageable intervals during class. Do students want the chance to listen

TABLE 1.1 Practical Ideas for Bringing Fun into Learning Experiences for Students.

Ideas to Use Humor	*Ideas to Use Novelty*
Use a Joke of the Day and invite students to share cheesy jokes as well. Fun riddles also work well.	Once you have established a routine, switch things up at times to incorporate preferred activities on occasion.
Tell students about the things that make you smile and invite them to share the same. Laugh at yourself often!	Surprise students with a random funny hat or costume related to the content. Most students love this at all ages.
Sprinkle in funny pieces of media, such as YouTube clips, to bring laughter and lightness into the classroom.	If something isn't working, change it! Think outside the box with your approach and try new things.

Ideas to Offer Preferred Activities	*Ideas for 'Gamelike' Learning*
Survey students on their interests and preferred activities outside and inside of school.	Use a spinner wheel for student selection, either from a board game or online at www. wheelofnames.com.
Create a class-wide agreement to incorporate these preferred activities during class.	Intersperse odd trivia questions that connect with your content.
Incorporate student interests in the lesson whenever possible. Get creative and invite them to share ideas on how to do this.	Utilize the formats of popular game shows such as *Jeopardy* and *Family Feud* to review content.

to music while working using headphones? Create an agreement to allow this practice with proper parameters. Perhaps students like to learn through videos and visuals. Incorporate these whenever it is humanly possible.

As a special education teacher, you also have a real-world life of your own outside of school, and this shows up in how you orchestrate learning spaces. You have an agenda for your instruction, which includes learning outcomes you hope to accomplish each day. I have found that the most successful learning spaces involve the merging of the students' needs, preferences, and interests with the teacher's goals, hopes, and desires. In order to bring these varying perspectives to light and find commonality, I use an activity called Your Likes, My Likes. This is a Venn diagram which helps us create agreements on how everyone's needs and priorities will be met. The process of creating a Your Likes, My Likes agreement looks something like this:

1. Take some time early in the formation of your group or class to hold a 'meeting.'
2. Using a Venn diagram (see Teacher Tool 1), ask students to brainstorm the things they need and like in a school experience. Students often list things like 'nice teachers,' 'technology,' and 'free time.' Then, list the things which are important to you as a teacher, such as 'student learning,' 'good student attendance,' etc.
3. Discuss where you can 'meet in the middle' to create a fun and productive learning space. Write your agreements in the center of the Venn diagram. In the past, this area has included things like 'five minutes of free time at the end of class,' 'focused learning time,' 'limit distractions,' and 'technology breaks.'
4. Post the agreements in your classroom and invite students to sign them. I usually created a poster-sized version with space for student names.
5. Reference the Your Likes, My Likes poster and update it as needed over the course of the learning experience. Try to meet the needs students listed while also implementing your goals for learners.

The Your Likes, My Likes exercise has been particularly useful in classrooms where my perspective and student perspectives differed. Offering the Your Likes, My Likes experience demonstrated that I cared about their needs, preferences, and interests, and it wasn't all about me and my control. The Your Likes, My Likes offers the opportunity to come together as a cohesive community.

Another way to send the message that you care about your students and you want to meet their needs may involve tools to bring out their individual perspectives. This may support you in bringing in desirable elements to help engage students. Surveys can help you learn about the elements of each student's real-world interests to better get to know them and meet their needs in the classroom. Teacher Tool 2, My Favorites, is designed for use with students at the elementary level and Teacher Tool 3, What Matters to Me, is designed for use with students at the

Teacher Tool 1: Your Likes, My Likes

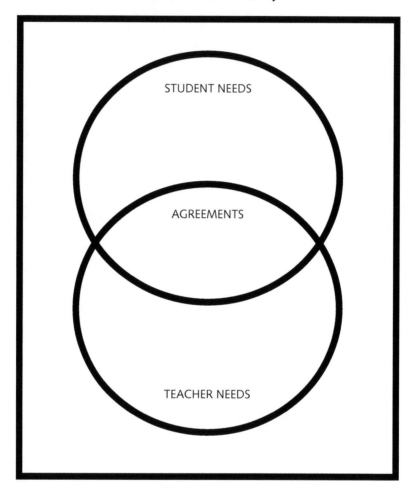

Teacher Tool 2: My Favorites

Name: _____   Date: _____

Tell me all about your favorites, your dreams and your best moments!

1. Favorite Things _____
   _____

2. Favorite People _____
   _____

3. Favorite Pets _____
   _____

4. Dream Job _____
   _____

5. Favorite Places _____
   _____

6. I Like it When Teachers Are: _____
   _____

Teacher Tool 3: What Matters to Me

Name: _____   Date: _____

Answer the following questions to help your teacher learn about what matters most in your life.

1. What do you value most in your life?

   _____

   _____

2. Who are the most important people in your life?

   _____

   _____

3. What traits would you have if you could be anyone you wanted?

   _____

   _____

4. What is your dream job?

   _____

   _____

5. What are some accomplishments you are proud of?

   _____

   _____

6. What is the highlight of your life so far, or your best moment?

   _____

   _____

7. What qualities do you look for in a friend?

   _____

   _____

8. What gives your life meaning?

   _____

   _____

9. If you didn't need to make money, what would you do with your time?

   _____

   _____

10. Describe your dream teacher- what do they do? How do they act?

_____

_____

11. Describe your dream class at school. What would it look like?

_____

_____

12. What can I do as a teacher to help you like school?

_____

_____

secondary level. This tool may be particularly useful for students whose interests outside of school differ greatly from the school world. You may use information from the survey to further exercise empathy when students share aspects of their vision for an ideal life context. Bringing the school world and the student's out-of-school life together may help you reach even the most reluctant learner.

> Bringing the school world and the student's out-of-school life together may help you reach even the most reluctant learner.

You will notice that the surveys include questions about a student's ideal teacher. Inviting feedback on teaching style can be a bit humbling, but this is actually a good thing. This demonstrates the openness and caring students need in order to trust the adults in their lives. It tells the student that learning is a shared experience and that you aren't in their lives to be an authoritarian ruler. I have always loved the concept that my job as a special education teacher is to participate as a co-creator of a future successful adult. We are partners with the same goal: the student's lasting success. This perspective is energizing and inspiring! I let students know that we are in this together, and we are sharing the responsibility for their learning. It isn't 'I will teach it, and you will learn it.' It is 'We will figure things out together.' I have found that for many students, this is a new version of the teacher-student relationship which really makes a positive impact! I hope you enjoy using the following tools to learn more about your students and take action accordingly.

Empower Students

> In the world of special education, the idea of success is going to look completely different for each individual student.

In certain circles, the concept of success is a synonym for wealth. In the world of sports, it's the best statistics. In the theater, it's a sold-out show with a standing ovation to top it off. For pop stars, it's record sales. For chefs, it's a good review. For computer technicians, it's a functioning system. The idea of success is relative and highly contextual. There is no one metric to define it, and everyone has their own version in their minds. In the world of special education, the idea of success is going to look completely different for each individual student. Many have tried and failed to create sweeping definitions of success for students (such as scores on standardized tests), but no single tool can measure the myriad of ways a student can succeed. For one student, it may be tying her shoes on her own. For another, it may be engaging in an impromptu social conversation. For another, it may be showing up for school every day for two consecutive weeks. This is part of the magic of special education. In our practice, we get the chance to look at a student as a whole person, not just a set of numbers on a testing report. We have the chance to help them imagine what true success looks like and then empower them to move toward this vision.

Academic success is important, certainly, but too often our students receive the message that if they don't naturally and easily understand the content, there is something wrong with them. Students respond by trying to avoid academics to protect themselves from further pain, frustration, and embarrassment. Far too many students have developed defense mechanisms to manage the difficulties they experience at school. A defense mechanism is a strategy used to ward off threats and reduce anxiety, and people often employ them without even realizing it (Ewen, 2014). Essentially, students lose who they are in the face of stress. They've lost their joy, and they spend their school day in an uncomfortable state of 'red alert,' looking for the next problem. In special education, we can help them find true peace in the school setting, bringing them fun and enjoyable experiences.

For example, a student who struggles with reading may act out in English class because they'd rather be seen as rebellious than incapable. As a special education teacher, you might try to build a trusting relationship with the student, helping them see success in a different light. The goal is to help students find pride in who they are, even if school doesn't come easily to them. Table 1.2 offers suggestions for ways you can convey your investment in students in response to their defense mechanisms.

As students grow in self-acceptance, you can help them decide who they want to be in this world. Through empowering conversation and modeling, you can show them that they can find belonging and self-worth without using their old defense mechanisms. Students realize that they get back what they give out and that life is easier when they learn to get along

TABLE 1.2 Conveying Teacher Investment When Students Utilize Survival Strategies.

Common Defense Mechanisms Among Students in Special Education	How Special Education Teachers Can Convey Investment in the Student
Refusing to attempt an academic task to hide the fact that they do not have the skills to complete it.	Discreetly encourage the student to give the task a chance and express how much you believe in their potential.
Testing limits with new adults to determine whether or not they are trustworthy. This may involve questioning teachers, defying teachers, or even insulting teachers at times.	Stay calm and consistently kind while expressing boundaries as needed. Build a relationship with the student by noticing their preferences and interests. Understand that trust can take time.
Taking long breaks in the bathroom or walking around the building when they feel overstimulated, overwhelmed, or stressed during class.	Discreetly chat with the student about their needs and set up a plan for them to take short, succinct breaks when needed. Teach coping skills to manage stress.
Rocking in chairs, tearing up paper, chewing pencils, or other physical activity which may distract others. This may be related to sensory needs or a desire for movement.	Offer movement breaks or the option to stand in the back of the classroom when needed. Provide fidget items to support sensory needs, such as small items to squeeze. Allow the student to chew gum.
Pretending to be capable of academic skills in order to avoid working on them and facing difficulty. Students may deflect targeting certain skills and accept low scores in these areas.	Continuously express how much you care about the student and believe in their potential for success. Build trust so that they show you their real, true selves, inviting them to take academic risks.

with the people who surround them both inside and outside of school. The opportunity to empower students who have been hiding their true selves behind defense mechanisms is one of the things I love most about my work in special education!

Students are astute, and they can sense when someone genuinely cares about them. When we approach teaching as an act of love, we show up ready to convey true investment in our students. We can show them that we are 100% on their side in the journey to make school a positive place. Students come to understand that they have someone in their corner to help them fight through the obstacles that have created difficulty in the past. Special education can give them a fresh start and help them see themselves and their school experience with new eyes. It doesn't need to be a stigmatizing life sentence to joyless remedial classes in the basement. We have the chance to empower them and celebrate who they are! We can help them realize that they are fully accepted, that everyone has issues to deal with, and that they don't have to keep their guard up at school any longer.

There may be nothing more rewarding than seeing a student transform from lost and struggling to peaceful and engaged in the school environment. A person at peace can live in harmony with other people, grow in integrity, and develop a positive identity. Once we help students establish the person they want to be, everything else falls into place. Academics improve because students become more willing to take risks and invest themselves in new challenges. Relationships improve because students don't have to use their old defense mechanisms to push people away. I have seen this happen many times, and it's an absolutely beautiful thing!

> When we approach teaching as an act of love, we show up ready to convey true investment in our students.

Help Students Write a New Story

As human beings, each of us is trying to make sense out of the world around us. We create stories to help us understand the world, and we live as the main characters in our own narratives.

Our students have their own internal stories which guide their perceptions of the world. The stories they are telling themselves may actually dictate their potential for success. So much in life is determined by what individuals believe about themselves. According to Robert K. Merton, a self-fulfilling prophecy is 'a false definition of the situation evoking a new behavior which makes the originally false conception come true' (Lopez, 2017). This phenomenon rings true for students today. What they believe about themselves often determines what they become. Too often, they hold false beliefs about their capabilities and sell themselves short, and this prevents them from fulfilling their full potential. They are telling themselves stories which hold them back from success.

As a special education teacher, my first mission is to get to know each student in my sphere of influence and identify the limiting stories they are telling themselves. After a bit of connecting and digging, I've discovered that nearly every new student I meet has some version of a negative, limiting story about themself. 'I'm no good at school.' Limiting story. 'I have a disability, so I won't ever be able to succeed.' Limiting story. 'I'm just not good enough.' Limiting story. 'I'm afraid of the future because I probably won't succeed.' Limiting story. These limiting stories are most often serving as self-fulfilling prophecies in their lives which keep them stuck. Over the years, I came to view these limiting stories as opportunities rather than problems. This was my chance to help students see that the stories which limit them do not hold truth and do not have to dictate their words, thoughts, and actions. One of my favorite aspects of special education is the chance to invite students to WRITE A NEW STORY!

In my practice, the process usually follows a similar pattern. First, I spend time building rapport and trust with the student so that they are willing to openly share with me. Second, we explore their current perspective on school and their past struggles in order to uncover any stories which may be limiting them. Third, we talk about a new, more optimistic story which focuses on overcoming past challenges, capitalizing on strengths and hope-giving beliefs. Finally, we work together to make the new and better story come true. Over and over and over again, I have seen this process TRANSFORM my students. It's absolutely amazing. In fact, this may be the single most powerful element of my practice which keeps me teaching special education year after year. Helping students write a new story is a beautiful act of HOPE both on the part of the special education teacher and on the part of the student.

> Helping students write a new story is a beautiful act of *HOPE* both on the part of the special education teacher and on the part of the student.

One of the most important things we can do for students is to give them hope. But here's the thing, we can't give away what we don't have. I encourage you to decide early and often that you are going to stay hopeful even for your student who is facing the greatest difficulties. As you begin to explore the limiting beliefs students are holding, you may be surprised at how hopeless and dire the situation may seem. Even in these difficulties, I have learned that with love, care, and thoughtful intervention, we can bring out the best in every individual. Some days, keeping hope alive is the toughest part of the job. On such days, we can say to ourselves, 'My best is enough.' Your best effort is all you can bring, and this is a daily act of hope.

Often, when people hear that someone is a special education teacher, they tend to say something like: 'Oh, you must have the patience of a saint.' This sweeping generalization is often far from accurate, but the sentiment is somewhat correct. When it comes to special education, patience takes on a different form. We create a plan to support the student, implement instruction, and then wait to see if it works. Many times, this involves repetition and reteaching, reteaching, and more reteaching of the same concepts. Patiently waiting for things to stick is an act of hope. Our work is not for the faint of heart, and we do indeed need patience to hold on to hope that their efforts will pay off for the student. We require the tenacity to hold on to the belief that what we do will have an impact, even if it is the tenth, twentieth, or fiftieth time they return to a key concept.

With hearts full of hope and a commitment to care for our students, we can unlock the new stories which will cause them to find success. The self-fulfilling prophecy can work both ways. Just as a negative belief may come true, a positive and hopeful story can come to fruition when we persuade students to believe in it with their full hearts. Teacher Tool 4: My New Story helps

Teacher Tool 4: My New Story

Name: _____

Complete the following sentences:

Past Negative Thinking:

1. In the past, I have struggled with _____
   _____

2. When I am at school, I have never really liked _____
   _____

3. At school, I have worried about _____
   _____

My New Story:

1. I believe that I will overcome my struggles by _____
   _____

2. I have many strengths and I am capable of _____
   _____

3. I believe that I will _____
   _____

you walk through this hope-giving process with students. The future dividends may be success for the students beyond previous limited expectations.

Strengths-Based Practice

Over my years in education, there has been a lot of talk about the importance of focusing on student strengths and incorporating them in our work. This seems to be a commonsense approach to helping our students feel capable and valued in our learning spaces. The problem? While there is plenty of talk about strengths-based practice, we continue to function from a deficit model in special education. The system requires proof that a student isn't succeeding, and too often, their strengths fall by the wayside, eclipsed by their many difficulties. The same can happen for us as teachers. At times, the difficulties of our work can cause us to forget what we are good at. We have much to offer our students, and we do well to remember this fact!

> Tapping into a student's area of strength may offer the perfect inroad to engagement in day-to-day learning experiences.

With regards to students, we can always start with something they are good at or an asset which already exists within them. The strongest instruction will include a hook or anticipatory set to elicit student engagement. Tapping into a student's area of strength may offer the perfect inroad to engagement in day-to-day learning experiences. This can create a shift from a deficit mindset to one of celebration and gratitude. You can invite students to share their strengths by posing questions such as, What skills or tasks come easily to you? What do you like most about yourself? What are your best characteristics? and What are you good at? Bring in versions of these questions during lessons and find ways to connect them to your content, and boom! You are executing strengths-based instruction. Students will bask in the glow of a focus on their most successful areas.

As a special education teacher, there is a good chance you also feel beat down and disheartened by the job at times. A focus on your strengths and assets can help you enjoy your day and your work, just as this can assist your students. Just as you work to uncover the nuanced strengths of your students, you can seek out and examine even your most subtle positive attributes. Now, there is something to be said for humility. Taking pride in who you are and what you are good at has nothing to do with ego and arrogance. Stand on your successes and let them be a beacon of hope for you in times of challenge. See Teacher Tool 5 for an activity titled My Strengths as an Educator that you can complete for yourself in order to identify and utilize their positive attributes. Hang onto this document and celebrate who you are. You have much to offer, and you will be happier in your job if you believe in your own capability and competence!

Teacher Tool 5: My Strengths as an Educator

<u>Positive Attributes:</u>

Five characteristics which help me in the classroom include:

1. _____
2. _____
3. _____
4. _____
5. _____

<u>Hope-Giving Beliefs:</u>

I believe I can share hope with my students by:

_____
_____
_____

<u>Celebrations:</u>

If times get tough, I can stand on successes from the past such as:

_____
_____
_____

<u>Lasting Rewards:</u>

My work has an impact on my students in the following ways:

_____
_____
_____

Conclusion

The most powerful factor which will sustain you in your work is the belief that you are making a lasting positive impact on your students. Tend to your sense of hope and believe in your effectiveness, and you will find that your motivation and love for the job increases tremendously. Create fun and productive learning spaces with your students in which they can heal from past pain they have experienced in the school environment.

Explore what matters to them outside of school, and find ways to merge it with your own. Offer students a new definition of success which accounts for their many unique strengths and abilities. There is so much more to life than a test score or a letter on a report card.

See your students as individuals who have the potential for greatness, and help them write a new story for their lives. Too many students limit themselves with negative stories about their potential. You have the chance to give them a completely new outlook, helping them embrace school as a place where they can succeed with the right support. Explore the many strengths your students possess and leverage these every single day. Also, remember that you are a strong, capable educator with numerous positive characteristics to offer. Give yourself a daily pep talk in which you choose hope over cynicism. Hope in the seeds you are planting. Believe in the growth that is happening among your students whether you get to see it immediately or not. Trust me, you are transforming lives every day when you show up with love and true commitment to realizing lasting rewards!

Simple Snapshot

- ◆ Know that you are planting seeds every single day.
- ◆ Accept the fact that students need to have fun at school.
- ◆ Teachers and students like and need different things— meet in the middle!
- ◆ Redefine your concept of success.
- ◆ Help your students write a better story for themselves.
- ◆ Recognize and celebrate your own strengths!

Reflection Questions

Use the following questions to reflect on what you have learned in the chapter. You may choose to journal about them or discuss them with a partner or small group to gain further insights.

1. Describe the legacy you hope to leave with your students. What are your goals for each of them?
2. What do you find most rewarding about your job in special education?
3. How might you sustain your hope in the possibility that each student can be successful?
4. How do you personally define success, and how does this influence your teaching practice?
5. How might you use student strengths to help students write a new story?
6. What are some of your strengths as a special education teacher, and how might these help your students?

References

Ewen, R. B. (2014). *An Introduction to Theories of Personality*. 7th edition. Hove, East Sussex, UK: Psychology Press.

Lopez, F. (2017). Altering the trajectory of the self-fulfilling prophecy: Asset-based pedagogy and classroom dynamics. *Journal of Teacher Education*, vol. 68, no. 2, pp. 193–212, doi:10.1177/0022 487116685751.

Wubbolding, Robert E. (2015). The voice of William Glasser: Accessing the continuing evolution of reality therapy. *Journal of Mental Health Counseling*, vol. 37, no. 3, pp. 189–205, doi:10.17744/ mehc.37.3.01.

2

Let Go of Perfection

It was the first day of school, and those first-day jitters she remembered from childhood had come back to her as she prepared to return to the classroom as a special education teacher. Ms. Ermeko would be working with students with emotional/behavioral disabilities to help them gain social skills and make progress on goals and objectives on their Individual Education Plans. Her assignment was upper elementary, with a caseload of fifth-grade students.

As Ms. Ermeko drove to school, she couldn't stop smiling. That first day would be just perfect. She would make sure of it! She arrived at work two hours early and was the only teacher in the building. As she turned on the lights in her perfectly decorated classroom, she could almost feel the magical learning that would happen in that room today. She would expertly get to know each and every student, forming a deep and lasting connection that would change their future. She would transform lives for the better. She would change the world one young life at a time. Her lessons would be impeccable, her pedagogy artful, her classroom management empowering, and her philosophical foundation firmly in place.

Brimming with anticipation, she set up for the day, checked her email, double-checked that she was completely ready for her lessons, and then she waited. Perhaps she hadn't needed to arrive quite so early. Finally, the moment arrived, and she headed out to meet the students coming off the buses. As students filed off their buses, they

DOI: 10.4324/9781003322528-3

wore glowing smiles as they greeted their teachers and friends after the summer break.

Ms. Ermeko's first class was small, with only eight students in it. After reading the paperwork on each student, she learned that all students had a history of behaviors such as fighting, aggression toward peers, aggression toward staff, academic difficulties, etc. 'Nothing a little love mixed with engaging, perfect pedagogy can't fix,' she thought.

When the bell rang, she had two students in the classroom. Both eyed her up and sat as far from her as they could, leaning back in their chairs with folded arms. Within a few minutes, the remaining students sauntered in. Tardy on the first day? She wouldn't get upset. Maybe they didn't know where the classroom was. She'd be lenient for this first day. High expectations could start tomorrow.

So class began.

'Good morning. I'm Ms. Ermeko. This is my very first day as a teacher, and I'm so excited about it. This is going to be great. I have a lesson planned where we are going to get to know each other, and I hope it will be fun as well.'

'Another boring, lame lady who talks too much. I'm out.' The student left the classroom, slamming the door behind him.

The rest of the class cracked up. They were gone. Ms. Ermeko had lost them. Now what? Should she pursue the student who took off? Should she stay in the classroom and try to hammer down some respect? Should she laugh along with them? Clearly, the lesson plan that was all sunshine, rainbows, and butterflies was out the window. Now it was time to fumble through and survive.

Somehow, she did make it through that first day, week, and year of teaching. She learned very quickly that the idea of 'perfection' was completely pointless in her practice. She decided to replace her perfectionism with flexibility and a genuine focus on breathing life into her students. She saved herself many headaches and found a pathway to enjoy her life as a teacher.

> The journey toward lasting success in special education begins with one simple rule: Let. Go. Of. Perfection.

Ms. Ermeko's learning experience demonstrates that even the most perfectly laid plans can take a different course when implemented in reality. Special educators who expect perfection often discover that their work has become impossible. The journey toward *lasting success* in special education begins with one simple rule: Let. Go. Of. Perfection. There is no such thing as 'perfect' in the journey of a special education teacher. Wake up every morning ready to give it your best and expect things to be messy at times.

You are working with young human beings. You will love them, you will empower them, you will inspire them, and you will discover that sometimes their thoughts and actions make absolutely no sense. Your best-laid plans may blow up in your face at times. In these moments, say to yourself, 'Well, at least I tried.' And please, keep your sense of humor. Teaching itself is an imperfect art. Every individual teacher brings his or her own ideas, style, and personality to the table, and that's part of the beauty of this profession. Don't get hung up on whether you are doing it 'right' or 'wrong' because things just aren't so concrete in this job. Focus on the results you are seeing in your students. Are they engaging? Is there laughter in your classroom? Is anyone learning anything? Trust yourself. You've prepared, and you're ready for this. I'm guessing you believe in your students, so believe in yourself too! This chapter explores questions such as the following:

- ◆ How might you value progress over perfection?
- ◆ What are some approaches you can use to create connections with students as you share your imperfections?
- ◆ How might you establish your role as a teacher and case manager so everyone knows what to expect (including you)?
- ◆ What are some strategies you can use to let go of perfectionism and offer yourself permission to let go of stress?
- ◆ How might you and your students set up agreements on your expectations for each other?

Progress, Not Perfection

High personal standards? Good.

A professional and strong work ethic? Fabulous.

A staunch adherence to perfection at all cost? Not so great.

> Perfectionism works against special education teachers, and those who last find a way to hold themselves to a high set of standards without burning themselves out.

Perfectionists simply don't last long in the world of special education. They may be far more vulnerable to both emotional distress and physical health problems, which can impede their teaching and their ability to provide what their students need from them (Sirois and Molnar, 2016). Teaching in the special education setting is a complex, difficult, and unpredictable job, any way you slice it. Research has shown that special education teachers who struggle with perfectionism quickly leave the profession (Jones, 2016). Perfectionism works against special education teachers, and those who last find a way to hold themselves to a high set of standards without burning themselves out. Yet how does one who has high personal standards let go of the unreasonable ideal of perfection? I suggest a relentless focus on progress and regular celebration of the small successes which happen all the time in the world of special education.

Once upon a time I decided to improve my health. I had developed some unhealthy eating habits and become quite sedentary, and it was time to get myself back together. It wasn't vanity. I just really felt unhealthy and had low energy levels. The first time I worked out, I could do NOTHING. My muscles were weak, my cardiovascular system was shot, and a brisk walk down the street left me wheezing like an elderly pug with asthma. How did I handle the situation like a mature adult? I whined. I complained. I sulked. I called my best friend and told her I was going to give up and let myself go entirely. What did she say? 'Quit your belly-aching and focus on *progress, not perfection.*' SO WHAT if I could barely make it down the street today. Tomorrow it would be easier, and the day after that it would be even easier, and before long, I would be crushing my goals. The secret? Just. Keep. Going. To use the words of my best friend, 'Suck it up, Buttercup.' Wow. Harsh pep talk. But it worked.

The same applies in our special education practice. We often find ourselves feeling defeated. At times we hope to accomplish

Teacher Tool 6: Celebration Plan

Use this form to remind yourself to celebrate PROGRESS at regular intervals in your practice. Remember, strive for progress, not perfection!

Circle the times in the school year when you plan to celebrate progress:

Before an assessment	After an assessment	Midterm or progress reports	End of a grading period
Before a break from school	After a break from school	Mondays as students settle in	Fridays! The week is done!
Completely at random- Surprise!	Whenever you have a small win	A student reaches a benchmark	When you observe acts of kindness

Five ways I might celebrate:

Ways to treat myself (intangible)	
Ways to treat myself (tangible)	
Friends to celebrate with:	
Ways to celebrate with students:	
Ways to celebrate with parents	

> Celebrate every small win, every student's smile, every adjustment you make that helps, every new learning experience.

goals which turn out to be unattainable or more long-term than we realized. We can combat the stress this may cause by fixing our eyes on the progress students are making. Celebrate every small win, every student's smile, every adjustment you make that helps, every new learning experience. You are making progress every day, and you are growing. Keep reflecting, seek out the wins, and you will find yourself motivated and conquering obstacles beyond your expectations. Teacher Tool 6 provides a Celebration Plan to help you intentionally integrate celebration in your practice. When completing this plan, you may consider identifying progress in many different forms in order to recognize achievements. Examples may include the following:

◆ A student who previously struggled with attendance comes to school every day for two consecutive weeks.
◆ A student who has been reluctant to try a new academic task dives in and masters it.
◆ A student who has been struggling to connect with peers makes a new friend in their lunch period.
◆ A student who has difficulty with initiating conersations with their teachers asks for help in one of their classes.

Realize that there is ALWAYS something to celebrate if you examine your students' actions carefully enough. You may also reflect on your own accomplishments and celebrate them as well. Did you finish a task you were dreading? Celebrate. Did you connect with a super-reluctant learner? Celebrate. Did you get out of bed this morning and show up for school? Celebrate! Sometimes, we take what we can get!

Relationships First

In the world of special education, our first goal must be to build a relationship with every student. Each learner is unique, and we are responsible to get to know them as deeply as possible if we are to meet their needs. We also help students engage at a higher level when they trust us and know that we are truly cheering them on! Keep in mind that students are tremendously perceptive. They can sense when we are genuinely interested in who they are and when we truly care about their success. Being a relational teacher is a general disposition which conveys warmth, caring, safety, and the desire for true connection. This shines through in small acts: asking a simple question about how a student is doing, noticing a pair of new shoes or a haircut, chatting about favorite Netflix shows, and all the other side dishes we add onto the main course of our content. Relational teachers aren't always all business, and they realize that students aren't droids who are programmed to sit and absorb knowledge. Our students are human beings who need fun, laughter, belonging, and yes, love in order to thrive.

In the world of special education, building relationships can be a messy process, and again, there is no perfect strategy which works for every student. One of my favorite tools for quick and easy relationship-building is thoughtful and intentional self-disclosure. I maintain the practice of selecting pivotal experiences to share in order to help students understand their own lives. For example, my daughter was adopted from Ethiopia at the age of 2. The adoption process was arduous, involving piles of paperwork, visits to notaries, court appearances, and endless fees. However, enduring through the challenges resulted in one of the most meaningful relationships in my life. My daughter is thriving, and I believe we were meant to be. The lesson? Sometimes, the greater the challenge, the greater the reward. Going through the motions and jumping through the hoops can lead to unlimited positive opportunities. My high school students liken this to earning their diplomas. When I share about this experience, I invariably hear from students about their own journeys. At times, they share about their own journeys from faraway places. Other times they share about a challenge they have overcome. My openness invites them to open up, which helps me get to know them more deeply and better meet their needs.

In my experience, the more real I am able to be, the more open, honest, and engaged my students will be. When you begin to share information about who you are and your personal life, students begin to see you as real people with their own difficulties and struggles. We model resilience and self-efficacy through our stories. We also model our okay-ness with our own human imperfection. So how can you practice strategic sharing to improve outcomes for students? Consider the following tips when choosing to implement strategic sharing:

> In my experience, the more real I am able to be, the more open, honest, and engaged my students will be.

- ◆ Determine Your Boundaries: When selecting personal information to share, remember that appropriate professional boundaries are a must. Oversharing may make students uncomfortable and may get you into hot water with parents. Topic areas to avoid include details on your medical history, romantic experiences or mishaps, and anything related to religion. Wisdom is necessary to ensure respect for all students and for the unspoken code of ethics we practice as teachers.
- ◆ Identify Common Student Difficulties: Plan the stories you plan to share based on common difficulties you see among students. Perhaps you have a go-to story to help students manage their mistakes. Maybe there was a time you overcame an academic obstacle. These anecdotes can offer students helpful information from your experiences. Be real, be messy, be human, and students will connect with you more deeply.
- ◆ Build Safety and Trust: Establish and uphold the expectation that your classroom is a space of safety and trust. As you share your stories, expect that students will honor the idea that the learning environment is a safe space for sharing. By sharing your experiences, you are showing your students that you trust them enough to hold space for your stories. This is a beautiful way to invest in the relationship and invite them to trust you in return.

Teacher Tool 7: *Stories to Share*

Complete the following with short stories from your personal life that you can share with your students. Focus on situations in which you struggled or made mistakes but were able to overcome them. This shows students you are real and models perseverance and a growth mindset:

A time I set and achieved an important goal:	
A time I made a mistake and was able to make it right.	
A time when I felt a strong, overwhelming emotion and I handled it.	
A time when I was upset with someone and we made up.	
A time someone was upset with me and I made it right.	

♦ Avoid Bias: Consider the information you share carefully in order to root out bias. For example, when sharing about your family, make sure you don't convey a bias toward the structure you experienced growing up. Families are diverse, and students must feel valued for their own experiences as you share yours. Remove any details which may communicate a bias toward 'right' or 'wrong.' The intent of sharing is not to sway students one way or another, but rather, to illustrate positive messages for them to consider.

◆ Invite Reciprocal Sharing: As you share your stories, invite students to share in return. Student voices are the most important in your classroom, so keep your stories concise enough to allow time for students to reply with their connections. You may also utilize technology to welcome sharing if there isn't enough time for discussion. For example, after sharing a personal anecdote, I ask students to send me their own stories related to the topic via email or a Google Form. They seem to enjoy this, and we enter into a correspondence which is entirely designed to build our connection.

When we share about ourselves, we deepen our connections with students and invite them to share who they are. We create a space where stories matter. Inclusive education sends three key messages to students: 'I see you. I like you. And I'm glad you're here.' See Chapter 6 for more detail on this approach with specific strategies. One of the things I love about special education is that when students hear about our authentic selves, we get to learn about their beautiful stories and bring them out of their shells. So open up, share about your struggles and imperfections, and you will be leveraging them to help your students! Teacher Tool 7 provides an activity you can complete to plan for the stories you will share with your students to help build connections. Enjoy!

The Myth of the 'Perfect' Teacher or Case Manager

What makes a perfect special education teacher? Friends, there is no such thing. Your version of the ideal special education teacher is as unique as you are, and the same goes for your students. There are simply too many variables involved and too many hats on the heads of special education teachers to create a cookie-cutter version of perfection. You will be happiest when you identify your own set of standards and hold yourself to them, which we will help you create later in this book. It also helps to set up some simple practices you will complete in order to feel you are fulfilling the demands of your work.

> Rather than striving to be perfect in either role, continuously try to be yourself, be real, be caring, and be supportive!

In addition to delivering instruction, we also fulfill a highly valuable role in the lives of students and families: the case manager. Just as there is no such thing as a perfect teacher, there is no such thing as a perfect case manager. In fact, pressuring yourself to be both a perfect teacher *and* a perfect case manager may be a one-way ticket for a ride on the burnout train. Rather than striving to be perfect in either role, continuously try to be yourself, be real, be caring, and be supportive! Case management was once one of my greatest headaches. I used to think, 'You mean on top of teaching, I have to try to keep this family happy and help this student stay afloat when they aren't even with me and write the IEP and make sure the IEP is happening and monitor progress and . . .' You get the idea. I now realize that case management doesn't need to be a drag, and there are efficient ways to leverage this role to make a difference for students and families.

So how do I make the most out of case management while maintaining my sanity and managing my time? I return to the anthem of this chapter: let go of perfection and focus on the human beings involved! Case management is not about the most perfectly composed piece of paperwork or expertly orchestrated meeting. It is about offering a lifeline to a student and a family who needs it. It is about breathing life into a situation which was previously a total drag. It is another chance to bring light and warmth to your practice, and this pays off in better outcomes for the student and the family.

One of my most important tasks as a case manager is to win the trust of the family and the student. Once trusted, parents/guardians realize that I am there to provide support, and I am an ally, not an enemy, in the education process. Relationships with parents/guardians are explored more fully in Chapter 8 of this book. For now, realize that instead of being the perfect case manager, you can be one who is present and carries out the roles and responsibilities the family needs within specific parameters.

Teacher Tool 8: Meet Your Case Manager

Who am I?

Name:	Space for a Photo
Education:	
Hobbies:	
Contact Information:	
Favorite Quote	

What is my job?
- Have a meeting and write your Individual Education Plan:
  - We will talk about the things you are good at.
  - We will talk about how you are doing in school.
  - We will talk about the goals you want to work on.
  - I will write up a plan to help school go well.
- Help you out when you need it:
  - Talk with me if you need a change to your plan.
  - Talk with me if you are struggling in any way.
  - Talk with me if you need help with your work.
- Check in on how you are doing:
  - I look at your progress on your goals to help you.
  - I look at your grades in your classes.
  - I check in with parents/families often.

I am here to help! We are all in this together!

It is important to realize that parents/guardians and students have no idea what a case manager is supposed to do when they enter special education, or they have their own conceptions about this role. I suggest that you make your job crystal clear for them so that there is no confusion, and everyone knows the standard you are trying to live up to. In this way, there is no gray area, and you don't have to feel the pressure to be everyone's hero. **A case manager is not meant to be a savior. They are meant to be a support as the student figures out how to save themselves!** This is the ticket to lasting success. Teacher Tool 8 offers a form titled Meet Your Case Manager, which accomplishes two goals. First, it provides parents/guardians with a bit of information about the case manager to initiate relationship-building and perhaps help to identify some common ground. Second, it offers a clear list of case manager responsibilities so families know what to expect.

> A case manager is not meant to be a savior. They are meant to be a support as the student figures out how to save themselves!

You may utilize this tool in a variety of ways. I would suggest that you create the sheet at the start of the school year and distribute it to your caseload. You might choose to go over the sheet during meetings with families and students. The points on the bottom of the handout can help set forth parameters so that you can function within the boundaries of their roles. It can also help families and students understand when and how to access the assistance of their case manager. If you carry out the list on the bottom of the activity page, you are doing enough, and you don't need to feel pressure to be anyone's perfect hero. It's important to stick to these boundaries in order to prevent burnout, and you'll be better for everyone when you don't spread yourself so thin you become invisible.

My Job, Your Job

> We do best when we lay things out clearly for students, and we also help ourselves in the process.

Just as there may be many differing perspectives on the role of a case manager, students and teachers can also experience confusion regarding roles and responsibilities in learning experiences. Keeping in mind that there is no such thing as perfect, students and teachers can come together to define how things will play out on an ideal day for everyone. This takes the pressure off as it helps make everything clear and transparent. Research supports the idea that defining roles and expectations in the classroom can help everyone involved relax and enjoy the environment (Sprick, 2013). I truly believe that most problems students experience during the school day have a lot to do with miscommunication and a lack of clarity. We do best when we lay things out clearly for students, and we also help ourselves in the process.

My Job, Your Job (Teacher Tool 9) is a tool you can use to make things crystal clear for students while setting boundaries around your role. No perfection is needed, no superhero/savior/over-the-top rescuer role is required. You can simply show up and do your job, and students can do the same. There is a beautiful safety in that! You may choose to use this tool with a small group or an individual student depending on the situation. The conversation may flow as follows:

- ◆ What do you think the teacher's job is in the classroom (or small group)? (Note the students' responses.)
- ◆ Here are my ideas for my job in the classroom (or small group): (List the teacher's ideas for the teacher's role.)
- ◆ What do you think the student's job is in the classroom (or small group)? (Note the students' responses.)
- ◆ Here are my ideas for the students' job in the classroom (or small group): (List the teacher's ideas.)
- ◆ I am also your case manager. Here are my ideas about what that means: (List the responsibilities of a case manager.)
- ◆ I can help you as your case manager, but you will be responsible for many tasks on your own during your school day. Here are my ideas about what you will be able to manage by yourself, although you can always ask me for help if needed: (List tasks the student needs to complete or at least attempt without help, such as following their schedule, paying attention in class, attempting assignments, etc.)
- ◆ Identify tasks the special education teacher and the students will complete together.

This practice can help students to understand expectations. It can also guard against overhelping, as the special education teacher defines their role. Research has shown that overhelping students, or offering assistance they don't actually require, can actually lower their self-esteem and limit them (Nario-Redmond et al., 2019). Letting go of perfection means we can let go of the drive to overhelp, letting students shine on their own. Use the My Job, Your Job process to encourage independence as much as possible!

Teacher Tool 9: My Job, Your Job

My job in the classroom . . .	Your job in the classroom . . .
My job as your case manager . . .	Your job as a student . . .
Tasks we will complete together . . .	

Flexibility: Your Saving Grace!

Over the years, I have noticed that my happiest colleagues are also the most flexible. For the sake of your own joy and wholeness in your practice, I suggest you learn to be flexible too. Being flexible can be absolutely terrifying. For those of us who enjoy feeling in control, it can feel like falling without a parachute at first. Opening our minds and hearts and souls to the flow of the day isn't comfortable at first, and in fact, some find it terrifying. The underlying need for control can actually drive us into some pretty unproductive strategies as teachers. It can cause us to make up unnecessary rules, engage in silly power struggles, and cling to lesson plans which just don't suit our students' needs. The desire to control the world around us is often driven by fear of what will happen if we loosen up and let go of the reins. So I encourage you, special education teachers, to be fearless and see what happens. Most often your students will surprise you by engaging at a higher level when you loosen your tight grip on the classroom and let them be who they are.

In my years in special education, I can't recall a single day which unfolded entirely according to plan. The need for flexibility is one of the only guarantees I can think of in the world of special education. Flexibility is not an option if we want to stay happy in our work. Expect the unexpected, go with the flow, and know that you will rise to any challenge life can throw at you! Believe in yourself, special education teacher! You can manage whatever comes your way through flexibility, not perfectionism. As discussed in Chapter 1, you will have a great impact on your students when you build authentic, lasting connections with each of them. Flexibility is key in building a relationship with students and making sure their needs are being met. Students need teachers who are able to work with their needs in the moment and adjust plans accordingly. That's where we come in! We can approach our work with the knowledge that nothing is set in stone in the world of special education, and adjusting in the moment is an unavoidable part of the job. This means that we sometimes get to change the tire as the car speeds down the road—lucky us! However, if we see our job as an adventure and realize that at times we are just along for the ride, we can better enjoy the journey. We can be flexible and relational teachers who leave space for tangential conversations, following students down the rabbit hole, showing our students that we care about their interests and needs more than the predetermined lesson plan.

> Expect the unexpected, go with the flow, and know that you will rise to any challenge life can throw at you!

Perfectionism breeds rigidity. Why? Because in order to be 'perfect,' things need to fit within the tidy little boxes we have envisioned for our practice. Every individual in the classroom walks in with ideas on how they would like to experience their day, and flexible teachers can embrace student perspectives to help guide learning. When students recognize that the teacher listens to their input with regards to activities, they perceive that they are valued in the classroom environment. This bolsters positive relationships and subsequent teacher longevity in special education. Conclusion? You can seek out ways to incorporate flexibility and choice in the day to help everyone have a better experience. See Table 2.1 for examples of rigid versus flexible responses. Favoring the flexible response whenever reasonably possible fosters improved relationships with students and will help you stay sane in your work!

> Just as you are flexible and gracious to your students, there are many benefits to offering this same flexibility to yourself!

Just as you are flexible and gracious to your students, there are many benefits to offering this same flexibility to yourself! There was a time in my career when I was plagued by one of the most dangerous and exhausting habits a teacher can face: ruminating. I was the queen of all ruminators, and I obsessed over every little thing, especially my own actions and potential mistakes. I would replay every word I spoke after a meeting and think things like, 'I wish I wouldn't have said that,' or 'I should have said _____ instead.' If a student had a tough day or there was a negative incident, I would overthink my part in the chain of events, looking for where I might be to blame. It was as if I was seeking out my own imperfections and overanalyzing them. If you identify with this habit, I beg of you to please STOP! There

TABLE 2.1 Exercising Flexibility in Relationship-Building.

Situation	Rigid Response (Impairs Relationships)	Flexible Response (Fosters Relationships)
A student forgets their backpack at home with all of their belongings for the day.	Penalize the student for any late work which was in the backpack.	Provide what they need for the day or invite them to call home to get their backpack.
A student wants to go to the bathroom twice in the same class period.	Make them wait until the end of class because they have already left once.	Allow them a short break and reinforce that they need to complete all tasks for the day.
A student is having trouble making it to his classes on time because his locker is on the other end of the building.	Reinforce the importance of punctuality and mark them tardy.	Move the student's locker to a closer location to help them be on time for his classes.
A student is struggling in the lunchroom because there aren't any positive peers to sit with and eat.	Encourage the student to figure it out. They can get by eating on their own.	Invite the student to eat lunch in a chosen space and facilitate social connections in the lunchroom.

is a vast difference between reflection and rumination. Reflection is a healthy practice which invites you to think about what went well and what went not so great so that you can improve in the future. Rumination is an unhealthy indulgence which focuses on the negative, creates stress, and leads to burnout. So please, keep on reflecting, but avoid ruminating.

If you catch yourself falling down the rumination spiral, it may be time to shift your thinking. In these moments, give yourself FULL permission to let go of the particular task or issue. See Teacher Tool 9 for a Permission Slip activity you can complete to help you exercise flexibility with yourself. You may particularly consider the tasks in their practice which do not directly impact many students but which create 'mental clutter.' Feel free to let go of these areas to preserve your focus on what REALLY matters: student learning. This permission slip can be reproduced as many times as necessary. I hope it helps you let go of perfection/rumination!

Teacher Tool 10: Permission Slips

I give myself permission to let go of _____
_____
_____
_____
_____

If I find myself worrying about it, I will _____
_____
_____
_____
_____

Signed: _____
(Your Name)

I give myself permission to let go of _____
_____
_____
_____
_____

If I find myself worrying about it, I will _____
_____
_____
_____
_____

Signed: _____
(Your Name)

Conclusion

Let this chapter be a love letter to our imperfect, messy, unpredictable profession. Special education practice is rarely boring, and you will learn to live life on your toes. Trust yourself and believe in your ability to manage anything that comes your way.

Confidence is the key to your success with students. Let go of the perfectionist mindset and celebrate progress instead. Be who you are and bring your authentic self to your practice. There is no absolute 'right way' to do this job. There are too many variables involved, and the teachers who excel are flexible and find a way to connect with students. Expect the unexpected and adjust your approach to match your students.

Your decision to become a special education teacher is a beautiful, meaningful gift you get to give to society and your students. It does not mean that you have to put on a cape and become a superhero overnight. You are human. This means you have a lot to offer, but it also means there are limits to what you have to give. Define your role as a case manager clearly. Also help students understand roles and responsibilities within the classroom. Show up to love students, and everything else falls into place, even when things get messy. Perfectionism has no place in the world of special education, so write yourself a big, fat permission slip to be imperfect and sign it in permanent ink!

Simple Snapshot

- ◆ Value progress over perfection—both for yourself and your students.
- ◆ Relationship-building is our priority, and it is an imperfect process.
- ◆ There is no such thing as a perfect teacher or case manager.
- ◆ Defining the role of case manager can help make things crystal clear.
- ◆ Identify student and teacher classroom roles.
- ◆ Flexibility is not optional if you want to enjoy your work!

Reflection Questions

Use the following questions to reflect on what you have learned in the chapter. You may choose to journal about them or discuss them with a partner or small group to gain further insights.

1. What are some areas in which you struggle with perfectionism? How has this helped or hindered you?
2. What are some ways you might celebrate progress rather than perfection? How might celebration help your students?
3. How might it help your practice to define your role as a case manager? How could this help you let go of perfection?
4. How could the My Job, Your Job tool help you reduce your stress as an educator? Where do you plan to use this activity?
5. What is the relationship between relationship-building and flexibility? How might flexibility help you combat perfectionism?
6. Think about the Permission Slips activity. What would you write on your permission slip? How might you commit to letting this go?

References

Jones, Brady K. (2016). Enduring in an 'impossible' occupation: Perfectionism and commitment to teaching. *Journal of Teacher Education*, vol. 67, no. 5, pp. 437–46, doi:10.1177/0022487116668021.

Nario-Redmond, Michelle R., Kemerling, A., & Silverman, A. (2019). Hostile, benevolent, and ambivalent ableism: Contemporary manifestations. *Journal of Social Issues*, vol. 75, no. 3, pp. 726–56, doi:10.1111/josi.12337.

Sirois, Fuschia M., & Molnar, Danielle S. (2016). *Perfectionism, Health, and Well-Being*. Cham, CH: Springer International Publishing.

Sprick, Randall S. (2013). *Discipline in the Secondary Classroom: A Positive Approach to Behavior Management*. Hoboken, NJ: John Wiley & Sons, Incorporated.

3

Special-Educator Self-Care

As an elementary special education teacher, Ms. Scalia learned that she would be sharing students with a very seasoned, sweet, grandmotherly superteacher who had the most adorable classroom decor and materials she had ever seen, Ms. Henning. She had heard that Ms. Henning was like a living, breathing poster child for the archetypal awesome educator. Rumor had it, she only read books about the latest research in best practice. She experimented with ideas she found on Pinterest. She liberally spent her own money on securing resources for her students, and her whole weekend was dedicated to honing her craft, either preparing perfect lessons or writing detailed feedback for students to bolster their learning. She was essentially the quintessential 'perfect teacher.'

Ms. Scalia felt a bit of pressure to keep up with her partner teacher from day one. It was tough. She was coming into the classroom with the lessons she created for her methods classes in college. She was ready to learn and decided to see Ms. Henning as a blessing. Ms. Henning's proficiency was nothing to get intimidated about, after all, because this is a collaborative profession. Ms. Scalia knew she brought her own gifts to the table. Although she may not be experienced, she had a big, huge heart and lots of enthusiasm for her new job. Sometimes fresh eyes and ideas were helpful, and Ms. Scalia knew she could offer this as well. The pair was scheduled to spend an afternoon getting ready for the school year during the last week in August, and Ms. Scalia looked forward to it immensely!

DOI: 10.4324/9781003322528-4

The day arrived, and Ms. Scalia showed up early with pen and paper in hand to take lots of notes. Suddenly, the door flew open, and a vibrant woman with bright red glasses, short-cropped silver hair, and adorable red ballet flats paired with jeans and a white T-shirt flew into the room.

'Oh my goodness! I can't believe I made it here! There was construction at every corner, and I hit every red light! So here I am. Let's do this!' stated Ms. Henning in one breath.

'Well, hi there . . . so glad you're here . . . I've heard such wonderful things about you, and I'm guessing I could learn a lot!' Ms. Scalia stammered.

'Oh, honey, let that one go. You don't want to turn out like me! I'm on the verge of a nervous breakdown!'

'Huh . . . ? Are you serious?' Ms. Scalia felt confused.

'Listen. This job can eat your life. It has pretty much eaten mine! For thirty-one years I have done nothing but eat, sleep, and breathe special education. I've been obsessed. And let me tell you, it's time for me to let go. Every year, so much new stuff gets added to the plate, and I just give in to it and add it on to everything I'm already doing. Well, no more! I need to get a life! I almost couldn't come back this year because I'm feeling so burnt out, and that's just not fair to my students. So guess what. This year, I have one rule: Have FUN with the kids. That's it. I am going to have a blast doing this job and forget the rest. You with me?'

'Um . . . well, yes . . . I definitely want to have fun! I'm looking forward to loving the kids and building relationships!'

'EUREKA! She's got it! I've got news for you, sister: no one cares how cute your learning space is or how perfect your lessons might be. If you don't love this job anymore, it's time to get outta here. Burnout can definitely sneak up on you. If you learn one thing from me, learn this: you don't have to do it all and put on a good show. You just have to love kids and make sure they are LEARNING. I mean, that's the whole point!' Ms. Henning's eyes lit up as she spoke. 'I'm happy to be a resource to help you keep your sanity. Please learn from my mistakes!'

'Yes! Too funny! I'm with you 100%! Look, I'm a fast learner, and I have a lot to offer. Let's split up the workload as much as we can. It should be a great year!' Ms. Scalia felt energized and excited about her pep talk from the seasoned colleague. Ms. Henning would be an awesome resource she could turn to for support. Ms. Scalia knew that she could definitely love kids and make sure they were learning. If she woke up every morning with this mission, she knew she would stay happy and fall in love with her job.

And guess what? That's exactly what she did.

Ms. Henning demonstrates a mistake far too many special educators make: they neglect self-care and their personal time and allow the job to take over all aspects of their being. As so many of us have learned, this job can EAT YOUR LIFE. In fact, the more you love your students and the more you care, the greater the danger that this job will usurp your very existence. Yes, love your students. Yes, give your heart to this work. Yes, this means you must learn and practice the maintenance of boundaries to establish and sustain a healthy work-life balance. This chapter is loaded with practical, enjoyable activities to support you in setting boundaries, managing stress, finding wholeness, cultivating inner peace, and letting go of struggle. This may sustain you in your work and your life in general.

Anyone who enters the journey of an educator is someone I can respect. There are plenty of other jobs out there which are far less emotionally taxing and pay much better. You have made the choice to do something that really, truly matters. You are a gift to your students, although they may never let you know this. So value yourself and take good, loving care of your mind, heart, body, and soul as much as you can. The healthier you are as a person, the less you will struggle as a teacher. It's as simple as that. Students are incredibly perceptive. They can sense our best-hidden negative emotions, and I truly believe it can raise the stress level in the classroom. Finding your own deep sense of inner peace and taking confidence in who you are can help you create a calm, relaxed learning environment in which all learners can excel.

> The healthier you are as a person, the less you will struggle as a teacher. It's as simple as that.

We must find the answer to the question: what makes you happy? What's your cup of tea? What puts a skip in your step? What floats your boat? For me, it's a series of obvious, perhaps clichéd habits which just seem to work. I drink lots of water. I practice yoga (I know—it's not for everyone, and some of you just rolled your eyes). I get out in nature. I read books for fun, not just for pedagogical improvement. I drink good coffee with good people who make me feel good. I work out as hard or as gently as I want, as long as I'm moving my body as often as I can. These are just a few examples, and I'm not suggesting we all become yoga masters who read hundreds of novels. I'm just saying that you do well when you figure out your happy place and you get yourself there often enough to keep yourself centered, strong, and smiling. For a close teacher friend of mine, it's the golf course. For another, it's the basketball court. For yet another, it's reading literature featuring vampires and cheesy romance. For another, it's knitting. Yes. Knitting. Whatever your outlet, may you find it and enjoy it! Again, the more you love your life, the easier it will be to love your job and your students!

Just as you need to explore what makes you happy, you also need to figure out what stresses you out. What throws you off your course? What creates the most stress for you? What are your patterns which help and which are the patterns which don't help so much? It is so important to find a way of living in which you turn off the bad, focus on the good, and operate from a space of self-kindness. This chapter seeks to help educators to answer questions such as the following:

◆ What are your most common stressors and which resources work best to help you manage them?
◆ How might you shift thinking patterns to break free from unproductive thoughts and replace them with a healthy, productive mindset?
◆ What is self-kindness, and how might this have a powerful, positive impact on your life, health, and wholeness?
◆ When you do fall into negative emotions, how might you return to your center and repair any harmed relationships?
◆ How might you practice self-regulation strategies considering your own potential experience of dysregulation or trauma response?
◆ What is the role of mindfulness in self-care for both you and your students?
◆ How might you set boundaries in order to create a balance between school responsibilities and the joys of your personal life?

◆ How might you 'let it go' when things go wrong, leaving negativity and difficulty at school in order to reduce stress and struggle in your personal life?

Pairing Stressors With Resources

Okay. Let's just start with a simple truth: Special education practice can be STRESSFUL. Stress is unavoidable in the lives of special education teachers, but this isn't necessarily a bad thing. In some ways, stress may indicate that you care about your students and want to create the best possible educational experience for them. Stress becomes a problem when it erodes your mental health and happiness in life. Basically, a little stress is to be expected and may even be a helpful motivator. When that little bit of stress grows into a raging monster of anxiety, it creates a toxic situation, which isn't good for teachers or students. What is the solution? Figure out what sends you into that state of stress and overwhelm, and then identify the best solutions to combat the onset of such situations.

> Solution-based self-care will allow you to focus on the proactive steps you can take rather than the problems you face.

When you start reflecting on your stressors, it may be helpful to categorize them and identify which elements trouble you most. This can help you figure out the best strategy you can employ to deal with the things which impact you in each area. Always strive for a solution-based mindset, and try not to get stuck in the muck as you reflect on the things that weigh you down. Solution-based self-care will allow you to focus on the proactive steps you can take rather than the problems you face. As you consider your best stress-busting solutions, spend time creating a go-to menu of options you can turn to in challenging moments. Teacher Tool 11 provides an activity titled My Menu of Solutions you may complete in order to compile your favorite stress-relievers in various areas.

Teacher Tool 11: My Menu of Solutions

Consider your favorite coping strategies, self-care practices and resources. These may appear in this chapter, or they may come from past positive experiences. Complete the chart to create a menu of solutions you may utilize to sustain yourself as a special education teacher.

Area: Stress created by workload/deadlines.	
My favorite solutions in this area:	What will this look like in my life?

Area: Stress created by perceived lack of effectiveness.	
My favorite solutions in this area:	What will this look like in my life?

Area: Stress created by the needs of students.	
My favorite solutions in this area:	What will this look like in my life?

Area: Stress created by challenges with behavior.	
My favorite solutions in this area:	What will this look like in my life?

Area: Stress created by disagreements with colleagues.	
My favorite solutions in this area:	What will this look like in my life?

Area: Stress created by challenges with parents.	
My favorite solutions in this area:	What will this look like in my life?

Area: Stress created by personal difficulties.	
My favorite solutions in this area:	What will this look like in my life?

Self-Trust, Not Self-Doubt

From the day you were born, you started to take in information from the world around you. From before you could remember, you received messages about who you were supposed to be, what you were supposed to strive for, and how you were supposed to act. It's called life. We are all civilized by the influences of others. Sometimes, as we grow up, we find ourselves picking up some unhelpful thinking patterns and perceptions about ourselves. We internalize the message that we aren't quite good enough, so we lose touch with who we are. This creates stress and can hinder us in our practice as special education teachers. Self-doubt is one of the most harmful and venomous problems you will face as an educator, and if left unchecked, it could drive you right out of the profession.

So I implore you, in your journey as a special education teacher, find that true self deep down inside of you and CELE-BRATE it! The needs, preferences, dreams, quirks, flaws, ALL OF IT! Being completely at peace with yourself and delving into your deep well of inner confidence will make you a stronger person and teacher. This strength will carry you through any challenge you may face as an educator. Stop wasting time doubting your capabilities and decisions. Trust yourself and know that you want to do what is best for students and families. You have much more wisdom than you may realize, and this wisdom will only grow the longer you stay in special education.

> Being completely at peace with yourself and delving into your deep well of inner confidence will make you a stronger person and teacher.

For many years I struggled to trust myself in my practice. I knew the special education teacher I wanted to be, but I wasn't sure I was actually carrying out my convictions in real life. For me, I conquered this difficulty by figuring out exactly what I believed about teaching and about myself, and then taking actions in alignment with my own heart. For example, I knew I wanted to be a teacher who loved all students, but what did that really mean? It meant welcoming and accepting every single one of them. It meant putting myself in their shoes and viewing my lessons through their eyes. It meant bringing fun into the classroom so they could enjoy their time with me. From this level of specificity, I could implement new practices. I could affirm every student for exactly who they are. I could pre-reflect on lessons from the students' eyes and revise them to make them more engaging. I could make time for humor and plan strategies to incorporate fun on a daily basis with intention. When your actions match your words and your beliefs, you find who you are as a teacher, and self-doubt fades away. It's a beautiful thing, and it makes you fall even more deeply in love with our amazing profession.

Should you catch yourself falling into self-doubt, interrupt this thinking with self-encouragement and self-trust. You can always choose to cheer yourself on rather than question yourself and go down the self-doubt spiral. Own your decisions and remember that no one on planet earth is perfect (see Chapter 2), so you don't need to be caught up in potential mistakes. Think about your students who struggle with confidence and offer yourself the same pep talk you might offer to them. Remind yourself that you are competent, capable, and you are doing the best you can with the resources and tools you have.

Be Kind to Yourself

This leads to one of the most important tools a special education can employ to sustain themselves in the profession: self-kindness. If you work for a long enough period of time, you will make a mistake, which may create the need for repair. Too often, we act as our own worst critics, which can result in stress and emotional exhaustion. Learning to be kind to yourself and practicing this habit on a regular basis is an act of personal care, which can have a lasting positive impact on your overall health.

Too many of us spend our days being far too hard on ourselves, and this leads to a plethora of problems, including faltering confidence, inability to take positive action, and emotional pain. Research has established that one of the key causes of teacher attrition in special education is emotional exhaustion (Billingsley and Bettini, 2019). You will enjoy your life and your practice so much more if you learn to choose self-kindness over self-criticism every time! You have the power to take control of your thoughts, and you need to root out the negative as much as possible. You can choose thoughts which are kind to yourself, over and over. Not easy, but definitely possible if you commit to this practice with consistency. Special education is challenging, life in general can be overwhelming, and yes, you will rise to every challenge and sustain yourself better when you go easy on yourself!

> You have the power to take control of your thoughts, and you need to root out the negative as much as possible.

Too often, we become so lost in our difficulties that we forget that we possess a rich inner resource of personal wisdom. Teacher Tool 32, Letter of Kindness, offers a structure through which you may generate advice concerning difficult situations and use this advice to be KIND to yourself! When times get tough, be with yourself in a loving way, and care for yourself with gentleness and self-love. Those who make this a regular practice can face all the challenges of life with greater peace, including those involved in the work of special education.

The Power of Routine

Creating and practicing regular routines can be a powerful tool to help us avoid stressful situations. Managing the systems of daily life, such as meeting biological needs for food and rest, planning for clean clothing and reliable transportation, and other simple repetitive tasks can become draining when executed without planning or structure. No one thrives in chaos. Consistent routines may become lifesavers in your life as a special education teacher! It will help you so much as a special education teacher if you develop and execute regular routines which set the stage for smooth sailing through the day's schedule. Specific routine activities will vary from teacher to teacher, but overall, those who manage the systems surrounding their work in special education well experience less personal stress. As a woman who rarely turned on her oven or set foot in a grocery

Teacher Tool 12: Letter of Kindness

Consider a situation you are struggling with now or which has challenged you in the past. Imagine a friend or person you care about a great deal is in this situation. Complete the template below to compose advice to the friend. Then, re-read what you have written and take your own advice.

My Dear Friend,

I know you are going through _____

_____

_____

You have the strengths to handle it such as _____

_____

_____

Some words of encouragement I have for you are _____

_____

_____

Some new approaches you might try are _____

_____

_____

Sincerely,
Me

store for the first few years of teaching, I can attest to the importance of routine!

> No one thrives in chaos. Consistent routines may become lifesavers in your life as a special education teacher!

You might be thinking, YEAH, OBVIOUSLY! You may balk at the idea of reflecting on routines. I implore you, give this idea a chance. I have developed regular timelines for the menial tasks of life, from grocery shopping to laundry, and it has helped me tremendously! Rather than balking at the idea of a prescribed routine, give it a chance. Knowing my simple life routines and systems helps reduce the number of decisions I need to make, and I can simply walk out the steps of my day as planned. Everything gets done with far less stress than a life of pure randomness! Teacher Tool 13 offers an activity titled My Routines, which you can use to identify key tasks you may complete daily, weekly, and monthly as a part of their regular routine.

Teacher Tool 13: My Routines

Complete the chart to list key tasks you complete daily, weekly, and monthly. Then, add an estimated time for you to complete this and any additional notes to help yourself out!

What are some tasks I complete daily?	
Task:	Typical time and additional notes:

What are some tasks I complete weekly?	
Task:	Typical time and additional notes:

What are some tasks I complete monthly?	
Task:	Typical time and additional notes:

You may also identify when these tasks might take place, keeping in mind that any schedule also involves some flexibility in light of unforeseen events.

Leave It at School

When I was a brand-new special education teacher, I had very few other demands on my time. I was young and free, able to pour all my energies into the job which I loved. I remember showing up for school at the crack of dawn and staying for long hours in the afternoon, perfecting my craft. I wanted to put all my attention on the students during the day so I saved other things (like grading, paperwork, and preparing lessons) for my personal time. Sure, it cut into my hobbies, which at that time included drinking coffee with my friends and going to concerts until the small hours of the night. This wasn't such a big deal in this phase of my life. I could give and give and give to my job unreservedly, and it felt like I was doing the right thing.

As I continued as a teacher, life changed. I became a partner and a mom and suddenly I had people depending on me outside of just the people I cared for at school. I'm guessing you can predict what happened. I was so used to giving my whole life to my teaching job I neglected my other roles and had very little to give to my blossoming little family. Once I finally picked up my sweet baby from the childcare center, I was already spent. Things just weren't working, and I wasn't sure what to do. Teaching was and is my calling, so I wasn't going to leave the profession, but being a mom was infinitely important to me. I was frustrated, and I knew that my priorities were out of alignment, but I felt clueless as to how I could fix it.

So what worked for me? How did I survive? How am I still a teacher who wears a zillion other hats? Well, first I had to let go of perfection (please see Chapter 2 for details). Second, I had to realize that I had—let me take a deep breath before I say it—LIMITS. I am not Wonder Woman. Neither are you, or Superman, or whichever superhero you identify with most. If

I give all my time and love and energy to my teaching job, I have nothing left for my actual life. I thought about it this way, imagine a cup, whichever is your favorite. Mine is a coffee mug which says 'Rise and Shine and Make the Day Fine' on it. Love it. The cup is filled with your love, your time, your capabilities, your attention, etc. All day long at school you pour from this cup. Every time you share kindness with a student, spend time preparing a lesson, grade something, assist a colleague, attend a meeting, and so on and so forth. Once you hop in the car and drive on home, you might be pretty spent, and your cup might be on the empty side. How do you fill it up? Well, that's different for everyone. Maybe it's your relationships with your family. Maybe it's cooking a tasty dinner and snuggling in under a blanket to relax. Maybe it's taking care of your pet chinchilla. As mentioned, you know the things which fill you up.

Now, here's the point. Pay attention: the things that refill your cup must not be neglected! They are absolutely necessary or you are going to burn out on your special education teaching job before I can say 'Super-teacher.' Take the time for the things that refresh and restore you, and you will be better for your students. Trust me! I've learned from my mistakes. I had to find balance and learn to manage my time so that I could maintain a personal life even while being the best special education teacher I could be. It's completely possible when you keep your priorities in order.

> The things that refill your cup must not be neglected!

How about another analogy? I mean, why not. We've already compared our lives to a coffee mug. Another potentially helpful or potentially cheesy metaphor is that of two boxes. This actually helped me a lot when a teacher friend shared it with me early on. Think of your teacher life as one box and your home life as the other. When you are at school, you are only concerned with the needs, demands, and responsibilities of your school life. You're not thinking about that load of laundry you forgot soaking wet in the washer at home or whether or not you remembered to lock the back door. These things will be fine. You can't do anything about them anyway because you are at school. Focus on where you are in the present moment.

The same goes for when you are at home. Try not to obsess about the lesson you plan to teach tomorrow or the parent you have to call. Try not to check your school email constantly (gasp). Only concern yourself with the items in your home box. Again, this isn't easy for everyone, and it is a skill you may need to work on. I believe in you. I've lived it. I can't say I ALWAYS leave school stuff at school and home stuff at home, but I'm pretty darn close. It has really helped my sanity and my longevity in teaching!

One of the most important practices you can start now to sustain yourself in special education is to strike some sort of balance between work and life. I know, it sounds absolutely impossible because at times our jobs can seem impossible. I'm telling you, it is the road to happiness. Allow me to suggest some simple, practical strategies you may employ to protect your time away from school to the greatest extent possible:

◆ Set a 'stop' time each day and hold yourself to it! For some special education teachers I know, they give themself an hour. One hour to either tie up loose ends after school or to think about the events of the day. After that set stop time, they do not allow themselves to think about school to the greatest extent possible. When stop time arrives, change into a new outfit! Seriously! Sometimes I also take a shower if the day at school was particularly taxing. This helps me switch into 'home' and 'relaxation' mode.

◆ Learn to say NO! It is totally and completely okay to say this magical two-letter word, and the earth will not crumble if you don't join every committee, direct the school play, coach the track team, and cover for all your sick colleagues. If you say no, someone else will step up, so share the love, and don't feel you must take it all on!

◆ If you absolutely must work in the home environment, perhaps in response to a pressing deadline, keep your home workspace contained. As much as you can, keep your home a haven free from schoolwork. If you must work from home, use a space which is out of the way so you don't have to stare at your laptop or piles of paperwork all night long.

◆ To the greatest extent possible, compartmentalize your concerns and focus on school while at school and home while at home. For example, if you are struggling with a personal relationship, set aside these troubles while at school and focus only on concerns related to your students. If you are struggling with a coworker or student relationship, only think about these issues while at school.

Use Teacher Tool 14: My Boundaries to create a plan to support your work-life balance as much as possible. This tool may set the stage for less crossover stress between home and school..

Life-Giving Self-Talk

We all have a voice which speaks in our mind. It directs the path of our day and guides us along our path. Perhaps your voice is naturally kind and supportive. You believe in yourself, you are confident in every choice you make, and you never second-guess a thing. If so, you are probably the exception, not the rule. Far too often, the voice we use to speak to ourselves is too harsh, too extreme, and simply too much. This can wear us out over time. We must combat the negative messages which can play in our minds with intentional positive self-talk.

The way we speak to ourselves can come from our oldest memories. Some say that the voice in our minds will mirror the voices we heard from the adults who cared for us. If our caregivers were harsh and critical, we may be more critical with ourselves. If they were loving and nurturing, we have a better shot at being loving and nurturing within our minds. This tells us that we need to pay close attention to the voices we are imparting in

Teacher Tool 14: My Boundaries

Reflect on your use of time and energy by completing the chart below. Think about when you can take personal time to refresh yourself. Consider where you can say 'No' to avoid cluttering your schedule. Finally, reflect on how you can compartmentalize different areas of your life to manage the numerous 'hats' you wear most effectively.

STRATEGY ONE: My 'Stop' Time	
My goal 'STOP' Time:	My plan to stick to this time:
STRATEGY TWO: Learn to say 'NO'	
Tasks I have been asked to do which I could say 'NO' to:	Tasks I have said 'YES' to which I could delegate instead:
STRATEGY THREE: Compartmentalization	
Concerns I will only think about at SCHOOL:	Concerns I will only think about at HOME:

our students' life experience. We can be a loving presence for them to improve the likelihood they will be kinder to themselves in the future. This also tells us that the kinder we are to ourselves, the better we may be for our students. It's as simple as that.

In order to reprogram our minds and move away from negative self-talk, we must first become aware that it is happening. At times we may not even notice that we are being self-critical or negative. This begins with the simple practice of paying attention to our thoughts and our inner landscape in order to identify our problematic thinking. Once recognized, you can choose to focus on a better thought and send yourself an improved message. Over time this becomes a regular habit, which can breathe life into your overall health and your work as a special education teacher. See Table 3.1 for replacement self-talk for common negative thinking.

Another helpful practice is to start and end the day with positive messaging. Simple mantras can provide the perfect messages to get you going when you wake up. I like to spend the first five to ten minutes in quiet meditation on a few phrases which frame my mindset in a healthy way. It usually involves something like, 'I have so much to be grateful for today, I will show up and love my students today, and I have what it takes to handle any task

TABLE 3.1 Replacement Self-Talk for Common Negative Thinking.

Common Negative Thinking	Replacement Self-Talk
I am in over my head. I just can't handle this.	I have all that I need in this moment. I call upon my inner peace.
I always screw up when I do things like this.	I let go of past mistakes, and I know I am capable.
I know I need to let this go, but I just can't seem to get over it.	All is well. Time will heal the situation. I let go of things I can't change.
If I stop to rest, I will fall too far behind to recover.	I pause. I breathe. I rest in this moment. I deserve to rest sometimes.
Maybe I'm just not cut out to be a special education teacher.	I am exactly where I am meant to be. I am fulfilling a greater purpose.

which comes my way.' I like to engage in the same practice in the evening as well. Once my head hits the pillow and it's finally time for a good night of sleep, I move through a bit of thinking on what I'm grateful for. I remind myself of all that I'm grateful for with self-talk such as 'I did my best today, and I'm proud. I am completely at peace, and all is exactly the way it is supposed to be.'

> I have so much to be grateful for today, I will show up and love my students today, and I have what it takes to handle any task which comes my way.

Now, some of you may be cringing at the seeming silliness of these mantras. I know, it's not everyone's cup of tea. I would encourage you to give it a chance and see how your general mindset improves. See Teacher Tool 15 for an activity titled Morning and Evening Mantras, which invites you to identify phrases you can utilize to bookend your days with life-giving positive self-talk.

Conclusion

Take extravagant, fabulous care of yourself, embrace yourself, and LOVE yourself! The more whole and healthy you are, the better you will be in the classroom. Figure out what causes you stress and identify solutions to combat these triggers. Find your happy place and hang out there as often as humanly possible. Remember that your mind can play tricks on you and create problems which aren't actually there. Keep a close watch on the voice you use to speak to yourself in your head, and make sure your internal self-talk is SOAKED in kindness! The kinder you are to yourself, the kinder you will be to your students. Teaching can slurp up your whole life if you let it.

Learn and practice the magical art of setting and upholding boundaries. You don't need to say yes to everything, and if you do, you will burn yourself out. Set up healthy routines which are life-giving and support the ideal person you hope to be. As much as possible, leave school issues at school. This isn't easy at first, but it's very important. Keep your home a haven as much as you can. When you get home from school, put on some comfy clothes, take time to relax and decompress from the day.

Teacher Tool 15: Morning and Evening Mantras

Morning Mantras:
Choose from the following list or create your own.

I will do my best today.   I am capable and strong.   I am grateful

Today will be a good day.   Today is a new day.   Today I will love kids.

I have good resources.   I am enough.   I will walk in peace today.

1.

2.

3.

4.

5.

Evening Mantras:
Choose from the following list or create your own.

I did my best today.   I let go of any stress.   I celebrate today.

Today was a good day.   Tomorrow is a new day.   All is well.

I am loved.   I am valuable.   I am at peace.

1.

2.

3.

4.
5.

If you need to talk with someone in order to do so, consider calling a teacher buddy because non-teacher friends may not always understand your struggles. Develop a support system to help you release the day and enjoy your personal time free of school thoughts. Learn and repeat positive self-talk to set you up for a great day and end the day on a positive note. Commit to do whatever it takes to be your happiest, healthiest self!

Simple Snapshot

- ◆ Identify your stressors and plan strategies to cope with them.
- ◆ Learn to trust yourself more than you doubt yourself.
- ◆ Practice self-kindness and stop being your own worst critic.
- ◆ Develop and practice consistent routines.
- ◆ Leave school troubles at school and keep home troubles at home.
- ◆ Work on the voice you use to talk to yourself in your head.

Reflection Questions

Use the following questions to reflect on what you have learned in the chapter. You may choose to journal about them or discuss them with a partner or small group to gain further insights.

1. What are some of the most common stressors in your life, and what are some solutions you may employ?

2. How do you cope with extreme stressors in your job? Which are your favorite grounding techniques?
3. What advice would you give to yourself regarding the stress of special education?
4. What are some routines you regularly practice, and how do they help you?
5. How are you doing with setting boundaries? How might you use strategies such as saying no and compartmentalization to help you uphold a work-life balance?
6. How are you doing with your self-talk? What does the voice you use to speak to yourself sound like?
7. What are some positive phrases you can use to encourage yourself in the morning and evening? How about throughout the day?

Reference

Billingsley, B., & Bettini, E. (2019). Special education teacher attrition and retention: A review of the literature. *Review of Educational Research*, vol. 89, no. 5, pp. 697–744, doi:10.3102/0034654319862495.

4

Effective Decision-Making

The alarm sounded at 5:30 a.m., and Lisa Nguyen decided to hit the snooze and give herself a few extra minutes of precious sleep. After talking herself into crawling out of bed, she executed her usual morning routine, deciding what to wear, what to eat for breakfast, and what to pack for lunch. She decided to grab an extra layer because her classroom was often cold. She also noticed a few notifications on her phone and decided to check them. Her mom wanted to stop over for dinner. Would she be up for it? She decided to say 'sure' and texted her back. Her second notification involved a reminder about a bill she had to pay. She decided she would need to pay it today, but not right at this moment. She planned to pay it first thing after school. She decided to leave herself a sticky note reminder on the counter so she would not forget. Glancing at the clock, she realized it was time to hustle. She decided to leave her other notifications for later.

Hopping in the car, she debated with herself about the best route to take to school to avoid traffic. She decided on the roundabout pathway, which would avoid roadwork which had been creating delays. Ms. Nguyen made the last-minute decision to grab some drive-through coffee, selecting her drink and payment method. She chose to add an extra shot of espresso to give herself a little pick-me-up. By the time she had pulled into the parking lot at school, she already felt a bit tired. Why? Between waking comfortably in her bed and arriving at school, she had already made 15 decisions and counting. 'Well, on with the day,' she thought. With that, Ms. Nguyen headed into school

DOI: 10.4324/9781003322528-5

to make hundreds, if not thousands more decisions before the end of the school day.

> When we learn to make wise decisions as special educators, we can set the stage for increased student success!

Ms. Nguyen is not alone. Life is jam-packed with decisions from the moment we wake up in the morning to the moment our heads hit the pillow at night. It is estimated that an American adult makes 35,000 decisions a day (Sollisch, 2016). In special education, our decisions matter. Every single decision we make may have ramifications for the lives of students, may shape relationships with families, and may impact the work of other professionals. YIKES! The pressure! Yet there is a gift in this fact: when we learn to make wise decisions as special educators, we can set the stage for increased student success! This chapter will help you become a better decision-maker so that you can avoid common pitfalls in special education and improve outcomes for learners in your sphere of influence.

Through a combination of experience and logic, you will develop go-to approaches to various situations. You want to make sure that the go-to practices you embrace are best for students, best for families, and yes, best for your own sanity. My hope is that you care very deeply about your students, and you want to do what is best for them. When you make decisions from a place of genuine concern for student success, you may experience stress and pressure at times. This chapter explores strategies which may support you in making sound decisions with greater automaticity and less anxiety, seeking to answer questions such as the following:

- ◆ How might strategic priorities help with deciding how to spend precious prep time?
- ◆ How might organizational tools such as checklists help you decide what to do next with greater ease?
- ◆ What are some strategies you can offer yourself and your students to make better decisions?
- ◆ How might you share decision-making responsibilities with students to improve outcomes for all?
- ◆ What are your personal standards, and how might this help you make decisions with less rumination? How might you help students set standards for themselves?

Determining Priorities

First things first. It's a common saying with a very helpful underlying message: set your priorities in the correct order, and everything else tends to fall into place. I promise you that you will always have a to-do list in your work of special education. Just as you check something off, something else will pop up. For some, this can feel as though you are a hamster running on a wheel, endlessly expending energy and never reaching a destination. We must combat this type of thinking in order to sustain ourselves as special education teachers. Rather than thinking about the endless to-do list, we can set our sights on the most important tasks and take efforts to check them off. It's a great feeling to take care of the critical elements of our work knowing that we are helping our students with our efforts!

When you think about prioritizing, it helps to realize that taking care of the most daunting tasks first may actually be the optimal approach. Taking on the most intimidating item on the to-do list may result in an increased sense of accomplishment. Trust me! I know this may sound counterintuitive. Why not start small and work your way up to the big, important stuff? I believe that the best approach for prioritization involves identifying the most daunting, time-intensive tasks, executing them with vigor, and then leaving the 'easier' items for later. There is a natural tendency to procrastinate on the things we just don't like. Procrastination has the potential to trigger significant anxiety and worry because it involves the inactivity of piling up tasks, which can lead to overload and burnout, breeding fears, worries, and anxiety (Hughes et al., 2018). Yikes. Put simply, procrastination is not your friend, even though it can seem like a lovely idea at the time. That gnawing feeling in the back of your mind is the task you are avoiding, and this can steal your peace. The items languishing on the to-do list may become like a dripping faucet, constantly present and irritating.

> Setting clear priorities can help you avoid procrastination and manage time well.

Setting clear priorities can help you avoid procrastination and manage time well. When you set out to determine your priorities, always begin with the question: what is most important for the health, happiness, and learning of my students? Whatever impacts the most students most greatly should take on your focus. From here, it can help to have a strategic approach to prioritizing. When engaging in prioritization, you can systematically differentiate between tasks that are important and those that are urgent, as originally conceived by Dwight Eisenhower, thirty-fourth US president, who once famously stated, 'What is important is seldom urgent and what is urgent is seldom important' (Bast, 2016, p. 71). President Eisenhower developed a system for prioritization now commonly referred to as the Eisenhower Matrix for prioritization. See Table 4.1 for examples of how this matrix may be applied to your work.

When I find myself stressed by the many tasks I need to complete and the many encroachments on my time, I sit down and draw out this matrix. Then, I complete it in as much detail as I need to in order to make decisions on how to use my time. It helps me identify exactly where my focus belongs and where it does not. I often realize that I should be delegating something that I am taking on by myself, or that I am giving my time to useless activities which distract me from my goals. This simple exercise takes me about five minutes, and it can pay off in saved hours!

TABLE 4.1 Eisenhower Decision-Making Matrix for Teachers.

Important/Urgent: Do Immediately	*Important/Not Urgent: Schedule*
• Invest in building relationships with students • Paperwork which is due now • Grading/progress monitoring • Reporting incidents such as injuries or illnesses • Parent communication	• Lesson/unit planning • Paperwork which is due soon • Communication with other teachers • Training/debriefing with paraeducators • Family time/hobbies
Unimportant/Urgent: Do Later or Delegate	*Unimportant/Not Urgent: Eliminate or Limit*
• Organizing/Filing • Explore resources • Committees • Extra duties • Managing old emails • Social distractions (phone notifications, small talk with colleagues, etc.)	• Scrolling social media • Worrying and overthinking • Perfectionism • Gossip and drama • Decorating the classroom • Enforcing unnecessary rules • Power struggles

Develop a System

External tools such as checklists, calendars, folder systems, etc. can make a huge difference to our ability to manage our role. When we design organizational systems which work for us, we actually help ourselves make fewer decisions during the course of the day. How? We know what needs to be done next, and thus, we can invest our time accordingly. A teacher who is overwhelmed and juggling tasks like bouncing balls is more likely to make mistakes. Mistakes can actually increase our workload because we have to go back and fix the things we flubbed up in our whirlwind of activity.

> You will be so much happier and more peaceful in your work if you set up structure and organization for yourself.

You will be so much happier and more peaceful in your work if you set up structure and organization for yourself. Every teacher is unique, and your system may look starkly different from that of a colleague, but the fact remains that you need some type of process. There are a few simple practices I have learned which help reduce my need to make decisions and offer a safety net ensuring all tasks get done. These include the following:

◆ After replying to an email, I file it in a folder. This keeps my inbox relatively empty so I know which emails still need a response.

◆ I create the same file folder for paper documents on my students, which include the same key information, so I know exactly where to look when needed.

◆ I use a prioritized to-do list system which ranks tasks in order of importance based on upcoming deadlines. At times I also prioritize the items which will impact the most students.

◆ I create a paper calendar at the start of the year and post it on the wall with my full caseload and their IEP and evaluation due dates. I also note other key tasks, such as creating schedules, requesting transportation, and transition meetings in the spring.

Teacher Tool 16: IEP Planning Checklist

Preparing for the Meeting		
Objective	**Action Step**	**Check!**
Select the best time for the family.	Connect with parents/guardians.	
Create the meeting notice.	Include the time, place, purpose and list of attendees.	
Invite all participants.	Send the meeting notice to all attendees.	
Confirm attendance.	Send an email reminder the day before the meeting and call to confirm with parents.	
Gather key information.	Review progress on current goals and objectives and take notes.	
Prepare an Agenda.	Outline the topics you plan to cover in the meeting and create a note-taking form.	
During the Meeting		
Objective	**Action Step**	**Check!**
Get the meeting started.	Introduce team members and have them sign in. Share the purpose of the meeting and offer parents Procedural Safeguards. Begin by asking about student strengths.	
Gather key information.	Review student eligibility, parent concerns, assessment results, present levels of performance, areas of need, progress on prior goals, proposed goals, adaptations and educational programming,	
Make key decisions.	Does the placement suit the student? Is it least restrictive? Is there a need for related services, special education transportation, or summer programming? Are the adaptations appropriate?	

Articulate next steps.	Share the timing for IEP completion, review, confirmation and implementation.	
After the Meeting		
Objective	**Action Step**	**Check!**
Compose the IEP.	Transform meeting notes into the official plan. Make sure to keep it concise and avoid jargon.	
Share the IEP with parents/ guardians and obtain consent.	Send the plan to parents with the invitation for them to ask questions and request revisions. Obtain signatures indicating parent consent.	
Share the IEP with all service providers.	Disseminate the plan to stakeholders on a need-to-know basis (teachers, paraeducators, etc.)	
Implement the IEP.	Put the plan into place. Engage in frequent checks to ensure all services are taking place.	

◆ I create and use checklists to keep track of due process paperwork requirements. Teacher Tool 16 provides an IEP Planning Checklist, which simplifies the process and helps me decide what to do next. This helps to ensure I don't miss anything!

Guiding Student Decision-Making

Over the years, I have worked with many students in special education who want to depend on me too much. Some of them lack the confidence to take steps on their own. Others have learned that if they can get an adult to do the work for them, they don't have to take the risk or invest the effort to learn and grow. While this may be relaxing for them, the result is they learn nothing. As special education teachers, we must never do for a student what they could do for themselves. It's that simple, and this theme will repeat throughout the book. We want to

Teacher Tool 17: *Decisions, Decisions!*

Think about a decision you need to make. Complete the table to walk you through the DBED Strategy. You can use this strategy whenever you have a decision to make in your life!

D: Define the decision. What is the question you are trying to answer?	
B: Brainstorm possibilities. Make a list of all the ideas you may choose to use!	
E: Evaluate your list. Go over your list and highlight the best options. Write your favorites in this section.	
D: Decide and take action. Pick your best option and go for it!	

foster independence, and if we allow students to depend on us more than they need to, we will burn out! So consider this your invitation to let go of the need to overhelp in favor of student empowerment!

> As special education teachers, we must never do for a student what they could do for themselves.

This certainly applies to decision-making. Rather than making decisions for our students, we need to train them to engage in reflective decision-making on their own. Otherwise, we simply add to the thousands of decisions we need to make in a day. Also, I have found that whenever I make a student *for* a student, they usually don't like what I decide. Although they may not realize it, they like the driver's seat, and they are fully capable of taking the wheel of their own lives. Yes, even the little ones! Of course, we stay in the passenger's seat to guide them along and make sure they don't drive right into the ditch. It's a balance.

You can support students in their decision-making skills through explicit instruction in this area. Too often we assume that students possess the skills to make good decisions, and yet no one has ever taught them how to do this. We can equip students for improved lifelong outcomes when we set them up to make better decisions when facing a turning point or a problem. As adults, we are able to follow a series of simple steps in order to make decisions without even realizing it. This involves a form of situational analysis in which we reflect on all the variables involved and take action accordingly. We must help our students learn to do the same.

> We can equip students for improved lifelong outcomes when we set them up to make better decisions when facing a turning point or a problem.

This brings me to one of my favorite tools in my teacher toolbox, the DBED Strategy. Described in Table 4.2, this offers a structured decision-making process using the acronym DBED: define, brainstorm, evaluate, decide. Once students learn and practice this approach, they are better able to analyze situations, thinking in terms of cause and effect. Teacher Tool 17 offers an activity titled Decisions, Decisions, which affords students at any grade level the chance to implement the DBED strategy. The level of detail will vary based on student grade level and capacity for self-reflection.

Student Input Matters!

Happy special education teachers lead healthy, happy learning environments. In special education, this may mean that you are orchestrating a separate setting, instructing through small groups, engaging in co-teaching, or engaging in some other service model. When it's time to make instructional decisions, you will find yourself less burdened and more effective when

TABLE 4.2 DBED Decision-Making Steps with Instructional Tips.

Steps in the DBED Approach to Decision-Making	Instructional Tips for Sharing With Students
Define the decision: clearly identify the question you are trying to answer or the decision you are trying to make.	Students may experience stress when it's time to make decisions, which can cloud their thinking. At this stage, invite them to get specific about the situation.
Brainstorm possible options: freely list all possibilities without pausing to think them through or judge whether they are good or bad.	Brainstorming means freedom! Select the best modality for students based on their ability. Students who struggle with independent writing need the option to dictate their list to a scribe.
Evaluate each option: review the list and evaluate whether each item might be a good or a not-so-great option. Highlight the 'good' items on the list.	Provide highlighters for students. Support them in reading through their list and gently guide them toward the best course of action if they need assistance. Encourage independence.
Decide and take action: select your favorite highlighted item and take action. Remember that it's okay to go back to the list and try a different option if needed.	Students may need support in taking the first steps once they have decided what to do. Help them find the first baby step they may take toward the decision they have made.

you engage student input to the greatest extent possible. This deepens the empowerment we hope to provide for students, increasing their sense of self-efficacy as they are given say over their own experiences. When we set up our learning environments as dictatorships in which only the teacher holds the power to make decisions, we set the stage for our own stress and exhaustion. We invite power struggles, and we remove student voices. Essentially, we work against ourselves.

> When it's time to make instructional decisions, you will find yourself less burdened and more effective when you engage student input to the greatest extent possible.

How might we best share decision-making with students? In my experience, this needs to be a structured process which involves careful planning. The first step is our responsibility as teachers. We must open our hearts and minds to *hear* our students and actually open up to their perspectives. Learning to let go can be challenging, especially when working

Teacher Tool 18: Group Meeting Form

It's time for our group to make decisions on an issue affecting our group. Use this form to answer questions related to the best next steps!

Meeting Participants:		
Question	**Notes on Discussion**	**The Group's Decision**
Question 1:		
Question 2:		
Question 3:		
Summary: What will we do next?		

with high-need groups in special education. You may be wise to start small with strategies such as polling students, offering choices in activities, building ownership, and inviting students to prioritize their own learning topics from a menu of options. These approaches allow students to make choices without taking full control of learning situations.

In any group of students, whether a co-taught general education class or a small group intervention group, shared decision-making may take the form of a class or group meeting. You may hold a meeting whenever there is a decision to be made regarding the activities of the group or when there are issues which need to be resolved. The purpose of the meeting is to hear all options and perspectives, to listen to each other, and to arrive at a conclusion which works best for everyone. It's your job as the teacher to bring out all voices and make sure that everyone feels included. You also hold the task of guiding the group toward a compromise, which can be tricky but which can result in fantastic outcomes for students.

In order to increase the likelihood of successful class meetings, you can implement a few wise practices. Work with students to develop the group rules for these discussions based on the principles that all voices have value and all problems have solutions. At first, you will need to take the lead role as facilitators, but over time, students can learn to take the lead. This offers them a sense of ownership and fosters leadership skills. You will also need to help students to discuss their perspectives and reach agreements, especially in the beginning, but you can also step back over time and allow students to take the lead on these conversations as well. This helps students learn embedded social objectives such as listening to the perspectives of others, navigating disagreements, and reaching compromises. Teacher Tool 18 offers a Group Meeting Form which special education teachers at any level may use to engage students in making decisions as a group or class.

Set Your Standards

For many years of my life, I had no idea who I was or what I believed. My teaching career started very young, and in my early 20s I had just as much to learn about myself as I did about my students. As I worked on carving out my true adult identity, I found myself struggling in my special education practice with my ability to trust my decisions. I knew that confidence in my professional life was key, but I was often plagued by self-doubt after choosing a course of action. There were also plenty of mistakes in my early practice, which is a natural part of teaching special education, which only served to deepen my lack of self-trust.

Today I have learned to trust myself as a special education teacher. You will be much more relaxed and confident in your practice if you learn to trust in your ability to make sound decisions for your students. Self-trust and confidence are choices you can make. You can decide today to put aside self-doubt and stand by who you are and what you believe with the deep faith that you are doing what is right for your students. After making a decision, cast aside the temptation to question yourself and move forward based on the course of action you have chosen. You will stop wasting energy on useless thoughts, and you will be happier as a special education teacher.

> Taking the time to specify your standards in different areas may help with decision-making, as you develop your own sense of what is right and wrong based on your personal ethics.

One proactive step you can take now to improve your decision-making skills is to define your standards. A standard is a level of quality or achievement that is considered acceptable or desirable (Merriam-Webster, 2021). A set of clear, nonnegotiable standards were the missing piece of the puzzle for me when I was a young special education teacher. As I grew in my sense of self, I developed a clear understanding of my personal guidelines, and this helped me tremendously. You operate from your own set of standards for practice without even realizing it. Taking the time to specify your standards in different areas may help with decision-making, as you develop your own sense of what is right and wrong based on your personal ethics. Standards may be written as 'I statements' which function as commitments to oneself. Examples may include the following:

- ◆ I make sure every student I instruct is learning something daily.
- ◆ I support inclusion and helping students learn with their grade-level peers.

Teacher Tool 19: My Personal Standards as a Teacher

Describe your personal standards with regards to each area of your special education practice. Use them to guide your decisions.

Area	My Beliefs/Standards
Due Process Paperwork	
Relationships with students	
Instructional practices	
Interaction with parents	
Interaction with colleagues	
Advocating for students	
Work-Life Balance	
Personal health and wellness	

Teacher Tool 20: My Standards as a Student

Describe your personal standards when it comes to each area of your life. Use them to guide your decisions.

Area	My Beliefs/Standards
Schoolwork	
Friends	
Hobbies	
Sleep	
Eating	
Relationships with Teachers	
Relationships with Parents	
Personal Goals	

◆ I take care of myself and manage my stress to be a better person.

Once you identify a clear set of personal standards, you might utilize them to support decision-making with greater confidence and automaticity. The ultimate result may be less stress and decision fatigue, sustaining you in the profession. Teacher Tool 19 invites you to complete an activity titled My Personal Standards as a Teacher. As you set your standards, focus on your heart of love for your students and your commitment to bring them your best each day!

Just as you benefit from this practice, students may also set their own standards to help them make better decisions for themselves. So many students are tossed around my life, letting the actions of others or their circumstances dictate their course of action and decisions. We can help them define who they are and how they will make decisions by inviting them to set their own set of personal standards. Teacher Tool 20 offers an activity titled My Personal Standards as a Student, which may be used to help students define their own basic rules or guidelines for living. This can be so powerful as they move into the later years of their education and prepare to transition to adulthood.

Conclusion

It is an unavoidable fact that the life of a special education teacher is loaded with important decisions. This doesn't need to be overwhelming or stressful. Instead, see it as an opportunity to have a positive influence every day as you grow in your ability to make effective decisions. Invest careful thought in setting your priorities to meet the needs of your students and manage your time effectively. Systems and checklists can help you decide what needs to be done with greater clarity and less stress. This can also help you make sure you are thorough in completing required tasks, removing that 'Am I forgetting something?' feeling, otherwise known as self-doubt. In working with students, you can help them reduce stress by teaching them strategies to make better decisions. When students make better decisions for themselves, you will see them thrive and grow with less support. This is a beautiful thing and actually can alleviate stress for everyone involved (students, families, colleagues, and YOU!) Sharing decisions with students in your practice can also help them feel empowered and can make the school experience more enjoyable for everyone.

As you grow as a special education teacher, create a set of standards which dictate how you will operate from day to day. When your decisions come from a place of deep identity, you will trust them more, and you will experience less self-doubt. Know who you are and what you believe, and your decisions will flow easily from this place of confidence. You can invite your students to do the same as they develop their identities and move toward adulthood. Consider all areas of life in setting up standards and phrase them as 'I statements.' This powerful exercise may help both you and your students become more effective in making decisions.

Simple Snapshot

- ◆ You will make better decisions when you know your priorities.
- ◆ Developing checklists and organizational systems can reduce decision fatigue.
- ◆ We reduce our own stress when we help our students make better decisions.
- ◆ Involving student input in decision-making has fabulous results.
- ◆ Setting your personal standards can ease the decision-making process.
- ◆ Helping students set their own standards for living can help them make better choices!

Reflection Questions

Use the following questions to reflect on what you have learned in the chapter. You may choose to journal about them or discuss them with a partner or small group to gain further insights.

1. How do you set your priorities? What are your thoughts on the Eisenhower matrix?

2. What are some of the organizational systems you utilize to help you manage tasks and decide what needs to be done next in your practice?
3. What are your thoughts on the DBED strategy? How might you use this structure for yourself or your students?
4. What are your thoughts on sharing decision-making with students? How might you engage students in decision-making in your practice?
5. What are your challenges with decision-making, and how might you overcome them? Examples include overthinking, self-doubt, or lack of confidence.
6. What are your most important personal standards, and how do they influence your decisions?

References

Bast, F. (2016). Crux of time management for students. *Resonance*, vol. 21, no. 1, pp. 71–88, doi:10.1007/s12045-016-0296-6.

Hughes, R., Kinder, A., & Cooper, C. (2018). *The Wellbeing Workout*. Cham: Palgrave Macmillan. doi:10.1007/978-3-319-92552-3_60.

Merriam-Webster. (2021). Standard. In *Merriam-Webster.com*. Retrieved October 28, 2021, from https://www.merriam-webster.com/dictionary/standard.

Sollisch, J. (2016). The cure for decision fatigue. *Wall Street Journal*. https://www.wsj.com/articles/the-cure-for-decisionfatigue-1465596928.

5

Solace in Collaboration

Jacob Borden had always been a fiercely independent person. Growing up, he had learned to handle situations on his own, and he prided himself on his common sense and ability to read people. Jacob became a special education teacher so he could help students figure out how to be successful and independent just like him. He didn't expect that his life would be filled with collaboration with other adults. He found himself in constant communication and meetings with parents, colleagues, principals, itinerant service providers, social workers, psychologists, and the list went on. Sometimes it became overwhelming for him, and he wished he could just shut his door and teach.

One morning before school, a colleague, Gina Matheson, stopped by his office and asked to chat. Jacob tried to hide his irritation. He wasn't a morning person, and he had a few things to get done before the school day started. Gina was new to special education, and it was pretty obvious she was a little lost. Sometimes her constant questions wore him out, although he did like her take on student success. She could find the good in any kid, and it was kind of fun to see. He gestured for Gina to come in but kept his eyes fixed on his computer so he would seem busy. Hopefully, Gina will keep it short and sweet.

'I just wanted to let you know, I really appreciate working with you, and I've learned a lot about the math strategies you have been using in your group. Thanks for being willing to share with me . . . I see that you're busy, so I'll scoot. Just wanted to let you know.' Gina hopped up to leave the room.

DOI: 10.4324/9781003322528-6

'Gina, hold on,' Jacob said. 'Thanks for saying that. I know I'm not always a warm, fuzzy kind of person, but I really appreciate you too. You can see the good in any student, and it helps me see the good in them too. I've been here a long time, and sometimes I forget to look for the strengths in kids. You are really good at that.'

'Well, thanks for noticing! I really try to see the best in our kids because it helps me bring out the good in them. Glad I can actually help you because I'm learning from your experience every day.'

As Gina shuffled off to the copy room, Jacob smiled to himself. He realized that he had a lot to offer other professionals and that he could learn from them as well. He might be capable of handling everything on his own, but working with other teachers could help make the job more positive and fun. He didn't have a choice whether or not to collaborate, so he may as well enjoy it and make the most of the opportunities it could bring.

Mr. Borden recognized that in special education, isolation isn't helpful. Collaboration is built into the entire special education process, and this can be a source of learning, strength, and shared comfort for you. Our colleagues are even more important to those of us who work in special education as we depend on collaboration to coordinate services and ensure students' meaningful inclusion in general education (Billingsley and Bettini, 2019). When we learn and use practical strategies for effective, mutually supportive collaboration, student outcomes improve.

> Collaboration is built into the entire special education process, and this can be a source of learning, strength, and shared comfort for you.

No teacher is an island. No teacher is hanging out on a lonely beach surviving on coconuts and sending smoke signals for help. If a teacher were an island, that island would be populated by students, colleagues, administrators, department leaders, counselors, school psychologists, social workers, speech clinicians, secretaries, custodians, paraprofessionals, and the occasional instructional coach. This is even more true in the world of special education. We get to add on service providers, special education administrators, intervention specialists, and the list goes on. Thankfully, humans are pack animals. We thrive in community.

We have risen to the top of the animal kingdom thanks to our ability to communicate through the intricacies of language. Essentially, collaboration makes us all better, but in all honesty, it can also be a bit tricky.

If you've ever watched *Nature* on PBS, or maybe the National Geographic channel, or perhaps Animal Planet, you've seen that throughout the animal kingdom, there are pros and cons to functioning in a community. A lonely lioness can't take down an elephant, but a pack of fierce huntresses can launch a coordinated attack, which will have them feasting for days. A pack of wildebeests can outrun and confound a speedy cheetah, and you're only in trouble if you get separated from the pack. On the flip side, operating in a pack can also mean posturing for position and competing for resources at times. Watch a documentary about a wolf pack sometime, and you'll see that the animal kingdom can involve some nasty interactions within cohesive groups. So how do we take advantage of the interactive nature of teaching to avoid being a snack for a predator? We stay humble, we accept help, and we learn to listen!

This chapter explores tools and strategies you can employ to make yourself the best collaborator possible. We will seek to answer questions such as the following:

- ◆ How might we engage in mutually helpful relationships in which we benefit from the wisdom of others and also share what we bring to the table?
- ◆ How might we develop a support system to effectively support our work in special education?
- ◆ What are some ways we can communicate so others will listen and receive our messages?
- ◆ How might we refrain from seeming too passive or aggressive in our interactions?
- ◆ What is assertive communication, and how can it help us as special education teachers? How might it help our students?
- ◆ What is the difference between 'venting' and 'problem-solving,' and how can we choose to be positive in the face of shared difficulty?

As you dive into the chapter, open your mind to the value of collaboration. At times, it can seem like another burden added to our plates. No one likes an extra meeting, which seems like a waste of time. This chapter will help you realize that your colleagues may provide a rich resource to alleviate your stress and support your lasting success in special education.

We Don't Know What We Don't Know

When I first embarked on my journey as a special education teacher, I felt the pressure to be Sally Know-It-All. I put a lot of pressure on myself to dazzle everyone at my first special education teaching job. Part of the 'Rachel Show' was acting as if I didn't need any help. This was a mistake as I quickly learned that I didn't know what I didn't know. When you work in special education, you are a part of an established school culture with its own set of norms, unwritten rules, values, and priorities. You're also part of an established logistical system which dictates how you will complete your paperwork. You are a puzzle piece in a larger whole, and this means you must continuously learn from others and remain flexible. As soon as you master a computer system to complete your paperwork, the district may choose to subscribe to a different system. As soon as you master a particular curriculum resource, the district may mandate a totally different approach. In these moments, we can feel stressed and overwhelmed. Instead, see them as learning opportunities and tap into every resource at your fingertips to learn and grow. Stay you, be real, and be open to learning!

> You are a puzzle piece in a larger whole, and this means you must continuously learn from others and remain flexible.

Many special education teachers struggle to delegate tasks and ask for help. However, positive interdependence has positive results for students and is implicit in participation in a true team of educational professionals. I was certainly guilty of this at many points in my career. Today I realize that my colleagues and I can engage in healthy, mutually helpful relationships. I let go of my stubbornness, ignorance, pride, and concerns about 'looking

Teacher Tool 21: What I Bring to the Table

Identify the personal perspectives and assets you have to offer in the collaboration process.

BELIEFS AND PERSPECTIVES	POSITIVE CHARACTERISTICS
TRAINING AND EDUCATION	EXPERIENCE

clueless' in order to ask for information and help on a regular basis. Whenever I have the chance to help someone else, I do it! I have realized that there is MUCH that I bring to the table. The more I share and collaborate, the more willing my counterparts are willing to do the same. In the end, students win, and that's all that matters!

As you open yourself up to receiving help and learning the things you don't know, it may be helpful to reflect on all the strengths and assets you already possess. You have unique experiences and knowledge to help your colleagues and other stakeholders, and the more you can help others, the more fulfilled you will be. Teacher Tool 21 invites you to reflect on your personal strengths and assets through an activity called What I Bring to the Table. Have fun with this one! Celebrate what you have to offer and then share it with others to enjoy your work more deeply. Then, open yourself up to receiving help from others along the way when this becomes necessary, and I promise it will!

Find Your People

For nearly 13 years of my teaching career, I ate lunch with the same three people every single day. The four of us grew to be more than colleagues—we were also close friends. These incredible individuals inspired me and helped me grow tremendously as a special education teacher. They were a source of shared laughter, support, and creativity, which proved invaluable to my happiness as a special education teacher. When it was time to move on to new roles and other opportunities, we stayed connected and cheered each other on from afar. Collegiality is such a gift, and my hope for you, dear special education teacher, is that you also find your people in your current work.

> You will benefit greatly from the development of a network of resources.

You will benefit greatly from the development of a network of resources. It may help to think about key areas in your practice in which you may need support. In special education, we wear far too many hats to be the expert on everything. When we try to take on this role, we end up withholding valuable resources from

Teacher Tool 22: My Network of Resources

Select key areas of your practice in which you may benefit from support. Complete this document to save key resources in one place for easy access to help when needs arise.

Area:		
Experts I Know:	Online Resources:	Additional Resources:
Area:		
Experts I Know:	Online Resources:	Additional Resources:
Area:		
Experts I Know:	Online Resources:	Additional Resources:

our students. Too often, I have seen professionals in education develop a savior complex, in which they believe they are the sole champion who will be able to help a student. This is a one-way ticket to stress and burnout because we simply cannot do it alone. So please, let go of the idea that you are the 'chosen one' who will save the day for students all on your own. Love them, support them, and do all that you can. Then, enlist the help of a network of resources to make the outcomes even better. Teacher Tool 22 invites you to identify key support personnel, online resources, and additional resources you might utilize through an activity called My Network of Resources.

Assertive, Yet Kind

For many years I taught social skills groups for students in middle school with special education services in the area of emotional/behavioral disorder. I should mention that I really dislike that label, and I don't think it serves students well. In these groups, there was a huge focus placed on communication skills. Nearly all conflicts students experienced could be traced back to a problem with communication. We worked together on the idea of drama-free living based on effective communication skills. One of the first rules I asked students to set for themselves was a 'no gossip' policy. Easier said than done in middle school. Unfortunately, I have found that gossip also runs rampant among education professionals. The trouble is, when we talk about each other behind each other's back, it usually gets back to the person and creates conflict. Conflict is stressful, and I have seen it create huge strife for special education teachers.

So I implore you, rather than talking *about* others when there are minor rifts or struggles, talk *to* them about the issue with assertive kindness. Assertiveness is a form of communication involving a confident statement which expresses a point of view without aggressively threatening the rights of another or submissively permitting another to ignore or deny one's rights or point of view (Cayoun et al., 2018). Consider the common tale of Goldilocks and the Three Bears. In this classic story, Goldilocks finds herself tasting porridge, which is too cold, too hot, and then 'just right.' The same can be said of communication. Overly aggressive communication could be seen as 'too hot,' alienating others and standing in the way of the message. Passive communication could be seen as 'too cold,' causing the individual to shy away and fail to convey their message at all. Gossiping is both passive and aggressive because the gossiper neglects to share the message with the right person, and they tend to be very negative in what they share. Just. Don't. Go. There.

I assure you that if you develop the habits of assertive communication, you will garner more respect from your colleagues, and you will be a stronger collaborator. Say what needs to be said to the right person with as much kindness and diplomacy as possible. You will feel better when you get your message out rather than bottling it up. Your messages will be better received when you take care not to be too aggressive. An assertive communication style may be 'just right' to help you sustain positive relationships and flourish in your work.

> I assure you that if you develop the habits of assertive communication, you will garner more respect from your colleagues, and you will be a stronger collaborator.

You may develop an assertive communication style by engaging in self-reflection on your current tendencies with regards to interaction. Teacher Tool 23, My Communication Style, offers a reflection you may complete to identify your current communication tendencies and move toward assertiveness. This activity also involves scenarios which can help you imagine how you might respond in a passive, aggressive, or assertive way. Preference on assertiveness will serve you well in future communication.

Both students and teachers can benefit from learning to use assertive communication. When working to be assertive, the communicator never wants to make the other participant in the conversation feel accused or misjudged. This simply serves to escalate negative emotions and augment conflict. Using 'I statements' may help communicators share their perspectives without causing others to feel attacked or upset. Teacher Tool 24, I Statements, may be used with students to help them practice the ability to assert themselves most effectively. You may also benefit from using 'I statements' when communicating your perspectives with assertiveness.

Teacher Tool 23: My Communication Style

Complete this activity to reflect on your communication style and evaluate various scenarios to identify response options. Keep in mind that an assertive communication style may support your work as a collaborator and reduce the stress of conflict or passivity in your interactions.

Describe situations which bring out the three types of communication styles in you. When are you most Passive? Aggressive? Assertive?		
Passive:	Aggressive:	Assertive:
Consider this scenario: A colleague talks over you in an IEP meeting and you have to fight to share your thoughts. It has happened more than once- it's a chatty colleague. Describe the passive, aggressive and assertive response:		
Passive:	Aggressive:	Assertive:
Consider this scenario: A colleague repeatedly asks you to watch their class while they go to the restroom or make copies and it is cutting into your prep time. Describe the passive, aggressive and assertive response:		
Passive:	Aggressive:	Assertive:
Consider this scenario: A colleage has been loud and distracting in a shared office space. You find her enjoyable, but she is getting in the way of productivity. Describe the passive, aggressive and assertive response:		
Passive:	Aggressive:	Assertive:
Final Reflection: What tools or ideas might help you to cultivate assertiveness?		

Teacher Tool 24: 'I Statements' Activity

Read each story. Write an 'I Statement' you could use. Remember that the formula for an 'I Statement' is:

"I feel _____ when you _____. Could you please _____."

Someone keeps saying mean things to you at lunch.		
I FEEL:	WHEN YOU:	COULD YOU PLEASE:

A friend tells you that your shirt is ugly.		
I FEEL:	WHEN YOU:	COULD YOU PLEASE:

Your teacher asks you to do a math problem and you don't know how to do it.		
I FEEL:	WHEN YOU:	Assertive:

Another student steps on your toes in line and it doesn't seem like an accident.		
I FEEL:	WHEN YOU:	COULD YOU PLEASE:

You see someone picking on one of your friends.		
I FEEL:	WHEN YOU:	COULD YOU PLEASE:

The Trouble With Venting

As a special education teacher, you may have heard terms such as 'decompressing' or 'venting' referring to conversations about negative situations. There is a common conception in education that venting is a necessary part of a teacher's life in order to reduce stress and maintain sanity. While it may feel good to express negative emotions such as anger, sadness, or fear, dwelling on emotions may actually serve to make you feel worse, especially if you don't find a way to gain a positive alternative perspective. There is certainly some value in processing situations in order to find proactive solutions. However, venting in the wrong contexts can create many issues, including data privacy violations, broken trust among professionals, and increased attention to the negative aspects of situations. I find that venting feels like complaining and wallowing in the muck for me. I have learned to avoid these conversations and let go of the bad by intentionally shifting my mind back to all that is good after a tough situation.

> While it may feel good to express negative emotions such as anger, sadness, or fear, dwelling on these emotions may actually serve to make you feel worse, especially if you don't find a way to gain a positive alternative perspective.

When you spend time venting, you may think you are alleviating your troubles, but in truth, you may be adding more energy to the situation. Thus, the idea that you need to vent in order to manage stress works against your ultimate goal: moving on and feeling better. Yes, you need safe and trusting relationships in which you can be honest and express yourself. However, you are wise to sustain your commitment to respecting the privacy of students and focusing on the positive as much as possible. Sharing about the negative emotions may actually cause you to reexperience the pain, increasing the experience of anger, grief, or anxiety associated with the difficult incident (Suttie, 2021). Not the goal!

There is an alternative! You do indeed need support at times, and I suggest that you enlist a trusted professional as a solution partner, as opposed to a venting buddy. The hope is

Teacher Tool 25: Solution Partners

Rather than 'venting,' identify someone you could use as a helpful resource in each area. Choose individuals who can help you focus on solutions rather than problems.

Solution Partner for Student Academics:	Solution Partner for Student Academics:
When can I contact them?	When can I contact them?
Phone Number/Email Address:	Phone Number/Email Address:
Solution Partner for Student Academics:	Solution Partner for Student Academics:
When can I contact them?	When can I contact them?
Phone Number/Email Address:	Phone Number/Email Address:

that this person becomes a trusted confidant and source of positive support. I believe that building friendships at school and developing a support network helps special education teachers remain in the profession longer. The focus of a solution partner relationship is to discover strategies to solve problems rather than complain about them. The right relationship with a positive and uplifting colleague can sustain your heart and help you focus on solutions rather than adding energy to the problem. Teacher Tool 25 offers a form you may use to identify solution partners for various situations.

Conclusion

Let this chapter remind you that collaboration is a gift! It can be a tricky, complicated part of the job at times, but remember that everyone has the same goal in the long run: student learning. Never shy away from asking questions! It doesn't make you seem incompetent; it makes you seem like you care about doing things right. It can also save a lot of wasted time and energy because you won't have to go back and correct your mistakes. Embrace the countless opportunities for collaboration which will come your way. Develop a strong network and tap into their expertise often. Also reflect on what you have to offer and share it readily with colleagues.

With regards to communication, always avoid the pitfalls of gossip. Be direct, be open, be honest, and be kind! It's okay to speak up for yourself when you need to, but always try to use empathy and put yourself in the other person's shoes. How can I share my message in the way it will be best received? Choose to be assertive without being overly aggressive. Regularly using 'I statements' can help both you and your students. When it comes to recovering after a difficult or negative incident, focus on solutions and shift your mindset back to the positive. Rather than venting and complaining. which could get you stuck in the muck, enlist the support of a positive colleague to seek out proactive solutions and move on quickly. Your colleagues may be the best resource you have to sustain yourself for the long haul in special education, so please don't be an island. Be a part of the pack, and live in harmony with others to the greatest extent possible!

Simple Snapshot

- ◆ Asking questions is a sign of wisdom, and it doesn't make you a burden.
- ◆ Consider what you have to offer, and share your gifts with colleagues.
- ◆ Build a network of support and friendship as much as possible.
- ◆ Learn to communicate with assertiveness. Not passive, not aggressive.
- ◆ Using 'I statements' to share perspectives preserves relationships.
- ◆ Focus on problem-solving, not venting, when discussing your difficulties.

Reflection Questions

Use the following questions to reflect on what you have learned in the chapter. You may choose to journal about them or discuss them with a partner or small group to gain further insights.

1. How might the guiding principles of professional learning communities help you as a special education teacher?
2. What are some strategies you might use for effective collaboration? How have these been working for you?
3. What are your thoughts on 'assuming positive intent'? Do you find this helpful? Why or why not?
4. How might you favor assertive communication rather than being too aggressive or too passive? What are your strengths and challenges in these areas?

5. What has been some of your experiences with venting your frustrations? Do you believe venting is helpful and necessary? Why or why not?
6. How might a solution partner be helpful to you in the areas of student academics, behavioral support, assisting families in crisis, and your own personal health?

References

Billingsley, B., & Bettini, E. (2019). Special education teacher attrition and retention: A review of the literature. *Review of Educational Research*, vol. 89, no. 5, SAGE Publications, pp. 697–744, doi:10.3102/0034654319862495.

Cayoun, B., Shires, A., & Francis, S. (2018). Mindful communication skills. *The Clinical Handbook of Mindfulness-Integrated Cognitive Behavior Therapy*. Hoboken, NJ: Wiley-Blackwell, pp. 255–76, https://doi.org/10.1002/9781119389675.ch11.

Suttie, J. (2021). Does venting your feelings actually help? *Greater Good Magazine*. https://greatergood.berkeley.edu/article/item/does_venting_your_feelings_actually_help.

6

Wise Advocacy

Mr. Bradford decided to join the Staff Development Committee to have a voice in his school. As a passionate young special education teacher, he had a lot to say about issues in the school and the direction it should be going. He planned to be a warrior for systemic change in this antiquated institution. The Staff Development Committee would be one place to make his valuable voice heard.

The meeting first began, and the principal introduced him as the new member of the group. He was warmly welcomed. The principal then opened the floor for committee members to share ideas for staff development topics this year.

'If I have to go to one more training about grading, I'm going to scream,' said a woman named Ms. Peretti. 'I mean, it's just not that big of a deal. There's no reason to change the system which is already working. I like the way I do it, and that's final.'

Mr. Bradford was appalled! In one statement, Ms. Peretti had summed up everything that was wrong with education! He had to speak up.

'Ma'am, no disrespect, but what you just said is exactly the problem with schools today. We can't be satisfied with the way we've always done things! Are you trying to leave students behind? I mean, grading is our biggest chance to communicate with students and parents. How could you say you're sick of it and you just want to stay satisfied with the status quo? That's embarrassing, to be honest. I mean

DOI: 10.4324/9781003322528-7

wow. *Ridiculous. Honestly, you probably shouldn't even be on this committee.'*

Silence. An awkward sniffle from Ms. Peretti. She didn't say a word for the rest of the meeting and stared with great interest into her lap. No one else spoke either. It was as if the oxygen had been sucked out of the room. Finally, the principal spoke.

'Okay, everyone, that's enough for today,' said the principal. 'How about you all head to your classrooms to get ready for the day, and we'll meet again soon to discuss more ideas. Thanks for your time.' Everyone fled from the room as fast as they could.

A sudden wave of self-awareness flooded Mr. Bradford. He realized he had been too harsh, and he had hurt Ms. Peretti's feelings and derailed the meeting in one statement. Around lunchtime, he received an email from his principal. 'Please come see me after school.' Sigh. This wouldn't be good. He tried to focus on teaching that afternoon, but he was watching the clock and counting down the minutes to his conversation with his boss. Deep in his gut, he felt a sense of dread and regret. This was not fun.

After school, the conversation with his principal went just fine. He was politely asked to tone down his participation in the Staff Development Committee.

'During your first few meetings on any new committee, it's probably a good idea to do more listening than talking, to be honest,' his principal said. 'Also probably smart to try to play nice in the sandbox. You got a little harsh there.'

Mr. Bradford was completely humbled. He apologized profusely to the principal and Ms. Peretti. He learned that even when he felt impassioned and needed to speak up, he needed to do so with care, kindness, and empathy in order for his message to be heard.

Mr. Bradford meant well and had a fair point. However, his communication was too aggressive, and thus, his message was lost. Many special educators identify lack of administrative support as a difficult factor in their roles (Hagaman and Casey, 2018). Over the course of my career, I have worked with many different administrators with many different philosophies. While I always respected my principals and followed their directives, I didn't always agree with their decisions or approaches. This is to be expected. Some administrators have a different understanding of special education in general or specific approaches to behavioral intervention. Again, this is to be expected. As a special education teacher and case manager, we are tasked with advocating for student needs with our colleagues and administrators. Through the use of wise and strategic practices, we can best meet this challenge with little stress while preserving positive relationships.

In addition to advocating for your students, there will be times you need to advocate for yourself. For example, when I was facing a medical issue and couldn't manage my paperwork, I asked my administration for a half day substitute to get it done. While I didn't want to ask for this, I knew it was imperative to my personal healing in light of the medical issue, and thus, I took the step to ask for what I needed. This worked out very well, and in the end, I was glad that I asked. Neglecting to engage in self-advocacy can contribute to your burnout. Finding a pathway to effective advocacy may support you in sustaining yourself in the profession and gaining confidence in your abilities to affect positive change.

> When you discover an unmet need either in yourself or in the lives of your students, it may be time for wise advocacy.

It is widely known that special educators are faced with vast workloads which can contribute to emotional exhaustion (Bettini et al., 2015). Considering the many demands already placed on us as special education teachers, it is important to develop the ability to advocate for personal needs in a proactive way. Put simply, advocacy is the act or process of supporting a cause or proposal (Merriam-Webster, 2021). When you discover an unmet need either in yourself or in the lives of your students, it may be time for wise advocacy. We also have the responsibility to ensure that the IEP is fully implemented, and this can involve advocacy for students. This chapter will explore the advocacy process and provide tools and strategies to help create less stress and more results when it is time to speak up. Driving questions for this chapter include the following:

◆ How might you take proactive action to advocate before issues arise?

- ◆ How might you best meet your own needs as professionals?
- ◆ How might you best advocate for the needs of students without falling into personal stress?
- ◆ How might you communicate in order to ensure their message is best heard when advocating?
- ◆ When should you enact advocacy, and when might you refrain from speaking up?
- ◆ How might you best advocate for inclusion and the least restrictive environment for your students?
- ◆ How might you advocate for students in the transition process and offer them the tools of self-determination?
- ◆ How can you prepare students to advocate for themselves by cultivating self-determination and personal ownership over their lives?

Proactive vs. Reactive

So many problems we face in special education are preventable. However, we too often find ourselves in survival mode reacting to negative situations after they have already occurred. One of the greatest gifts experience has given me as a special education teacher is the ability to recognize common patterns among my students and colleagues. I can assure you that the month of September tends to involve a bit of a honeymoon period. I can assure you that the month of February is when the school year begins to feel long, and there is a dip in student moods. I can almost promise you that as the end of the school year nears in May, student energy levels tend to rise, and focus tends to dwindle. Recognizing the potential issues presented by these patterns can help me be proactive. I can expect changes in student moods in February and work more fun and enjoyment into my lessons. I can expect heightened energy levels in May and work in more calming activities to help students regain their focus as much as possible.

Consider potential problems which may arise and get creative with steps to mitigate them before they take place.

Your special education practice is as unique as you are. In order to be proactive, consider the outcomes you hope for and the

Teacher Tool 26: Solving Problems Before They Start

Consider situations in which you may need to advocate for yourself or your students. How might you solve potential problems before they start? Complete this form to identify specific proactive actions you may take to set the stage for success.

Potential Issue:			
Who could help?	What may be needed?	What will I communicate?	Why might this help?

Potential Issue:			
Who could help?	What may be needed?	What will I communicate?	Why might this help?

Potential Issue:			
Who could help?	What may be needed?	What will I communicate?	Why might this help?

obstacles which may stand in your way. Consider potential problems which may arise and get creative with steps to mitigate them before they take place. The hope is that you will feel more secure in your ability to manage future problems and you won't feel as if you are flying by the seat of your pants quite as much. This can also help you engage in necessary advocacy conversations in order to preemptively meet student needs. Using the tools from Chapter 5, select assertive communication to set the stage for student success. Teacher Tool 26, Solving Problems Before They Start, may help you identify problems before they occur and plan for the necessary steps you may take to set the stage for better student outcomes.

The Power of a Pause

I'm a fast thinker, talker, and replier. I have a lot to say (obviously), and I tend to react impulsively at times. Thankfully, I have a seasoned colleague who shares a simple bit of advice which has become a bit of a mantra for me: 'Slow down, Sunshine.' I cannot tell you how many times I have wanted to unsend an email or unspeak something I have said in a meeting because I spoke or replied too soon. Again this comes back to my listening skills, combined with a lack of patience. So I offer you the most beautiful piece of advice I may have to give in this book with regards to connecting with colleagues:

PAUSE.

STOP.

AND THINK BEFORE YOU SPEAK.

So simple. So beautiful. So difficult. Many of us go into special education because we are passionate about our philosophies, and we want to share our thoughts. We love our students, and we love our point of view about them. There are so many different ways to approach all situations in education; we are bound to have conflicting views and opinions. No matter how 'right' you think you are, it serves you well to take a moment and consider alternative perspectives. Take a moment to organize your thinking and figure out the best way to frame your point so that it won't create a rift. Try to remove emotions from the picture because they just tend to charge things up. Our big feelings can be our worst enemies at times when we are trying to collaborate and communicate.

Too often, the need to advocate for oneself or one's students elicits an immediate response from a special education teacher. This can create difficult situations when the impulsive response isn't the most thoughtful or diplomatic. You will save yourself negative consequences and stress when you stop to pause before reacting. This offers you the opportunity to check in with your emotions, identify the true issue, and take wise steps toward solutions.

> You will save yourself negative consequences and stress when you stop to pause before reacting.

Advocating for Teacher Needs in Special Education

One of my favorite children's books and Disney films is *Winnie the Pooh* by A. A. Milne (Methuen Publishing, 1926). In fact, I have heard it said that the characters in this work represent different categories of difficulty our students in special education may experience. Pooh struggles with his cognitive abilities, Rabbit has challenges with anxiety, Tigger has a touch of attention deficit hyperactivity disorder, Piglet has a speech fluency issue, and finally, we can't forget our dear Eeyore, who is a pessimist who could probably secure a depression diagnosis from a clinical psychologist. Over my years as a special education teacher, I have encountered many colleagues who suffer from Eeyore syndrome. Nothing is ever right. Every step forward elicits a comment about two steps back. These individuals tend to be cynical and tired of teaching. They may still love kids, but they are bogged down by the minutiae to the point that they can only complain. Often, the target of their discontent is their administrators or the paperwork demands—the aspects of the job they feel they can't control.

As a special education teacher, try not to fall into an Eeyore mindset. It's easier to do than you think. There will be little things that bug you. There will be big things

> It's amazing how a negative attitude can dissolve in the presence of a positive human being. Happiness is contagious.

that drive you batty. Don't let them get to you. No one really wants to hear it, and it brings everyone down. Every day you show up at school, you have the choice whether you want to help bring a positive mindset to the overall culture or bring everybody down with your negativity. Now, does this mean that you have to be in a great mood every day? Of course not. You're human, and you will have down moments at times. It does mean that you can do your best to flip the script when you are grumpy instead of spreading that Eeyore energy. If you are struggling, find a student who makes you smile or an upbeat colleague to chat with. It's amazing how a negative attitude can dissolve in the presence of a positive human being. Happiness is contagious.

Does this mean we shy away from advocacy and accept our roles as they are? Certainly not. It does mean that we fix our eyes on the good as much as possible. When the good could be better through wise advocacy, we take steps to make things happen and affect positive change. The important thing to remember is that we must be selective regarding the situations and needs we choose to advocate for. If we constantly advocate in situations which we could have solved for ourselves, we may find that our requests are ignored. Teacher Tool 27 provides an activity you may complete to determine what you would accept and where you would advocate in various situations. Use this to bolster your skills in wise advocacy decisions.

Advocating for IEP Compliance

> A well-written IEP which is fully implemented can be seen as a gift to our colleagues, to our students, and to families.

Students with special education services have been historically disenfranchised by the school system and society. Many students depend on our school system to find a pathway to lifelong success, but too often, the trail is overgrown with weeds of stigma, lack of resources, and antiquated practices. Students can find themselves lost in the wilderness without a clear way out. As special

Teacher Tool 27: Accept or Advocate?

Read each situation and describe the action you would take. Would you accept the situation or advocate for change? Explain your thinking to reflect on your personal advocacy skills.

Situation: An administrator has asked you to give up your prep time to take on an extra duty if you can. One of the lunchroom paraeducators is going on leave. You don't have time and you need to say no.	
What would you accept about the situation?	Where might you advocate for change and how might this take place?

Situation: An administrator decides to call an intervention meeting for a student on your caseload and you feel overwhelmed already. The last thing you want is another meeting on your schedule.	
What would you accept about the situation?	Where might you advocate for change and how might this take place?

Situation: An administrator lets you know that your office space needs to move due to a construction project in the building. This will be an inconvenience and you will have to reteach your students on where to find you when needed.	
What would you accept about the situation?	Where might you advocate for change and how might this take place?

Situation: An administrator shares information about another student during an IEP meeting which violates data privacy. You aren't sure whether you should let him know that this is a problem.	
What would you accept about the situation?	Where might you advocate for change and how might this take place?

Situation: An administrator asks you to invite an interpreter to a meeting for a family, but you aren't sure how to access this resource. You feel stressed about making sure this service is in place.	
What would you accept about the situation?	Where might you advocate for change and how might this take place?

Situation: An administrator implements a new grading policy, but you have concerns about how this will work for students with modified grading on their IEPs. You aren't sure how to adapt the policy.	
What would you accept about the situation?	Where might you advocate for change and how might this take place?

education teachers, one of our most important responsibilities is to work with a team to develop an Individual Education Plan (IEP) for each student that best meets their needs. Once the plan is written and parents/guardians sign off on it, it becomes legally binding. Our charge as special education teachers is to share the student's individualized plan and make sure all team members follow it. This might feel like stressful pressure, but in truth, life is easier for everyone when students are successful. A well-written IEP which is fully implemented can be seen as a gift to our colleagues, to our students, and to families. Following it means we are using a helpful tool, not adding a burden to anyone's plate.

Teacher Tool 28: *IEP One-Pager*

NOTE: This information is confidential. Store in a locked file cabinet.

Student: _____ Case Manager: _____

General Need-to-Know Information		
Area	**Key Information**	**Action Steps**
Student Strengths		

Goals and Objectives		
Goal Area	**Objectives**	**Who will monitor?**

Accommodations/Modifications/Testing		
Area	**Specific Adaptation**	**Who will implement it?**

In my practice, I have always encouraged all participants to see the student's IEP as an invaluable resource and to look at it in a positive light! Once a new plan has been written and made official, I share it as soon as possible. When sharing this information, I select only the individuals who need to know the details of the plan (general education teachers, service providers, and paraeducators) and encourage them to store it in a locked filing cabinet to ensure data privacy. I distribute the full IEP document, as well as a one-page summary with the key highlights to draw attention to key information. See Teacher Tool 28 for an IEP One-Pager which you can provide for general educators, service providers, and paraeducators at both the primary and secondary levels. This advocacy tool may help ensure that the plan is implemented with fidelity throughout the student's day. It's such an important and valuable part of our work!

Fostering Self-Advocacy and Self-Determination in Students

Fostering self-advocacy skills in students can be an inspiring and FUN part of our work as special education teachers. As students develop the ability to speak up for their own needs, they are better able to find lasting success both during their education and during their lives beyond the classroom. The term 'self-determination' refers to a combination of knowledge, beliefs, and skills that enable a person to engage in self-regulated, goal-directed behavior with autonomy, taking control of their own destiny (Lopez et al., 2020). Essentially, students who experience self-determination can make decisions regarding their lives and take action to carry out these plans. Helping students take charge of their own lives and find their own voices might be my very favorite part of the work of special education! No matter how impacted a student may be by their disability, they can always grow in their independence and self-determination.

When students know how to advocate for themselves, they are better prepared for lasting success in the big, wide world. This also takes the pressure off you as their teacher to serve as an advocate. When we empower students through instruction in self-advocacy and self-determination, we actually protect ourselves further

> When we empower students through instruction in self-advocacy and self-determination, we actually protect ourselves further from burning out.

from burning out. Students take charge and we can step back, relax, and watch them succeed. Of course, we are always waiting in the wings should they need our help. Most often, once they realize that they can thrive and they learn to believe in themselves, they are able to exceed any limiting expectations.

Supporting students in developing self-determination skills should begin very early in the education process. In my practice, this starts by helping students recognize their personal strengths and assets. Next, students must believe in their own potential. We can help paint a picture of what success might look like for them in adult life. One of the most helpful tools we can offer students is the ability to use positive self-talk, particularly when it comes to their futures. We can support students in future success by helping them learn to change the conversation within their own minds. We must teach them to be self-encouragers with faith in their own capacity.

One strategy you may employ is to help students own their futures and engage in self-encouragement by inviting them to write a letter to themselves. The idea is to teach students to recognize what is going well and to believe in the potential they hold for a bright future. When students compose a positive letter to themself, there are two moments of benefit: first, when they engage in reflection by writing the letter, and second, when they receive the letter later in the school year or later in life (Vogelsinger, 2016). Teacher Tool 29 offers an activity titled Dear Future Self, which students may compose to engage in positive thinking about the future. I have a colleague who uses this tool often with middle school students. She saves the letters and tracks down student contact information years later when students would be reaching graduation age. Then, she mails the letter to students whenever it is possible. Student feedback on this experience has been tremendously positive, and students enjoy receiving their own encouragement during such a pivotal time in their lives.

Teacher Tool 29: Dear Future Me

Write a letter of encouragement to yourself. Then, take all the steps you need to get yourself there. Don't be afraid to ask for help!

Dear Future Me,   Date: _____

Today, I am _____ years old. I am in _____ grade.

Some things I am good at are _____

_____

My favorite things to do are _____

_____

Some things I have learned are _____

_____

I am working on _____

_____

I believe that I can _____

_____

In 10 years I hope that I am ____-_____

_____

Sincerely,

Your Name: _____

It's All About Transition

As you hope to set the stage for future success in the lives of your students, it is important to help them successfully accomplish the challenge of transition throughout their educational lives. Moving from kindergarten to first grade? Transition. Moving from elementary school to middle school? Transition. Finding the right path after high school? Transition. Times of transition can be scary and intimidating for students, and I have seen it bring out some pretty tough behavioral responses. However, the presence of a loving, caring teacher can make all the difference. Here we arrive at another aspect of special education I absolutely love—the chance to be that supportive presence as students navigate transitions.

> When a student prepares for a transition and succeeds, they grow in their confidence and their belief in their own capacity.

In addition to our consistency and care, students need to be equipped with self-determination and confidence in order to realize success after transitioning from one setting to another. When a student prepares for a transition and succeeds, they grow in their confidence and their belief in their own capacity. Success begets success, so we serve our students best when we find avenues for them to accomplish their goals in any small ways. Students grow in motivation and feel inspired to continue on their path toward a positive adult life.

What is the goal of all our efforts? I believe that from the very first day of school, from the very first interaction with a teacher, the goal is to start building the skills and abilities necessary for the student to manage adult life on the other end of their education. Special education is the perfect place for this to take place because we get to tailor our efforts to the precise needs of the student. We have the opportunity to see incredible outcomes when we serve as advocates who fully leverage the resources available to meet student needs. Teacher Tool 30 offers a tool you can use with your students as they reach the later years of their education in order to help them define their path.

Teacher Tool 30: Where Am I Heading?

Complete this reflection to start thinking about your future. Remember that you are the person in charge of your life.

	Where I am now:	Where I want to be 2 years after high school:	People who can help me get here:
Education			
Work/ Career			
Living Arrangements			
Things about my future I am concerned about:			
Things about my future I feel good about:			

Conclusion

The role of the special education teacher includes the requirement that we advocate for our students and their families at times. We may feel overwhelmed by this role and avoid advocacy conversations. However, this means we may leave our students in the lurch without necessary services or resources. As with any other part of our job, we can view advocacy as an opportunity to help our students. We can see it as another means through which we can show them our care, concern, and even love. When we care about our students, we can easily make the effort to try to secure what they need. The plan we create along with their team can be a gift to everyone involved. It's basically a how-to guide to meeting the student's personal needs in the school environment. What could be more valuable to an educator?

Deciding whether or not to advocate for a need comes down to this question: is this something I could fix on my own, or do I need support or resources from others? If we can repair the situation on our own, we should do it. If we cannot, we should advocate. Better yet, we can teach students how to be their own advocates as they move through their education. This prepares them to take ownership of their lives and take charge of their own bright future. We will not always be there to help them, so we must teach them to help themselves. Through instruction and practice in self-advocacy and self-determination, we can prepare our students to shine and thrive in their futures. The culminating goal of education is to produce skilled, happy, self-sufficient adults. As we advocate for students, we set the stage for this goal to be realized. I can think of nothing more inspiring and rewarding.

Simple Snapshot

- ◆ Solve problems before they start through proactive action.
- ◆ Pause before responding, especially when big emotions are involved.
- ◆ If you can solve a problem on your own, do it! If not, advocate!
- ◆ Provide simple tools to help everyone adhere to the IEP. This is a MUST!
- ◆ Teach students to take the driver's seat in their own lives and advocate for themselves.
- ◆ Help students determine their own path in life and support their dreams!

Reflection Questions

Use the following questions to reflect on what you have learned in the chapter. You may choose to journal about them or discuss them with a partner or small group to gain further insights.

1. How might you develop a proactive approach to potential problems in your practice?
2. What are some key situations in your practice which may require advocacy?
3. How might you best advocate for your own needs? When might you need to advocate?
4. How might you best advocate for the needs of your students while protecting your own energy?
5. What are some strategies you might utilize to share student IEPs with other educators and make sure they follow its content?
6. What are some ways you may help students own their own futures and advocate for themselves?
7. How do you support students in preparing for transitions from one grade level or phase of their education to the next?

References

Bettini, E., Kimerling, J., Park, Y., & Murphy, K. (2015). Responsibilities and instructional time: Relationships identified by special educators in self-contained classes for students with emotional and behavioral disabilities. *Preventing School Failure*, vol. 39, pp. 121–8, doi:10.1080/1045988X.2013.859561.

Hagaman, J., & Casey, K. (2018). Teacher attrition in special education: Perspectives from the field. *Teacher Education and Special Education*, vol. 41, no. 4, pp. 277–91, doi:10.1177/0888406417725797.

Lopez, N., Uphold, N., Douglas, K., & Freeman-Green, S. (2020). Teaching high school students with disabilities to advocate for academic accommodations. *The Journal of Special Education*, vol. 54, no. 3, pp. 146–56, https://doi.org/10.1177/0022466919892955.

Merriam-Webster. (2021). Advocacy. In *Merriam-Webster.com*. Retrieved October 28, 2021, from https://www.merriam-webster.com/dictionary/advocacy.

Vogelsinger, B. (2016). Five engaging uses for letters in your classroom. *Edutopia.org*. www.edutopia.org/blog/uses-for-letters-in-classroom-brett-vogelsinger.

7

Culturally Responsive Special Education

When Sharon Robinson graduated from college with a degree in special education, she promised herself one thing: she would love her students. Sharon had struggled in school and received services in special education to support her academic gaps and emotional needs. Her family had moved 16 times between kindergarten and her senior year due to issues with her father's work and struggles to keep up with ever-increasing rental fees for their meager apartments. Teachers had tried to help along the way, but no one made much of a difference until her junior year. This was when Sharon met Ms. Aiken. She still remembered their first day together.

Shuffling into a new school in mid-January, Sharon was exhausted before the day even began. She was tired of being the new kid, tired of learning her way around a new building, tired of figuring out a new system, tired of not knowing what was going on in class. Her schedule said she had a class called *Personal Development* for the first period of her day. 'Sounds like a joke,' she thought. She found the classroom and had a seat among a small group of about six other students. Tucking her head into her hood, she put in her earbuds and turned up her music, ready to ignore everyone and get through the day. Glancing around the room, she noticed a sign on the wall which read as follows:

'I See You . . . I Like You . . . I'm Glad You're Here . . . Love, Ms. Aiken.'

DOI: 10.4324/9781003322528-8

'Well, that's corny, but it's kind of cute,' Sharon thought. As Ms. Aiken entered the room and introduced herself, Sharon found herself putting her headphones away and actually listening. Ms. Aiken was warm, friendly, funny, and she asked questions as if she genuinely wanted to know the answer. She didn't seem to be in a rush, and somehow her calm manner made Sharon feel calm too. By the end of first period, Sharon felt better about the new school. As she got up to move on to her next class, Ms. Aiken met her at the door.

'So, Sharon, how are you feeling about everything? It can't be fun having to start at a new school in the middle of the year. How can I help?' Ms. Aiken said. There was something in her eyes that seemed real, as if she was sharing Sharon's experience, and she truly wanted to make things better.

'To be honest, it sucks,' Sharon said. She was surprised to hear her own voice sharing about her feelings. Usually, she kept her mouth shut and tried to handle her issues on her own. Despite herself, she opened up to Ms. Aiken. 'I'm so tired of moving, and I'm sick of being put in these small classes. I don't even know why I'm here. I know you seem like a nice teacher and everything, but I really just want to be left alone. I'm just one of those people who doesn't like school, who doesn't get good grades, and I just want to get by so I can get out of here. Thanks for being nice to me, but don't waste your time.' Sharon felt the lump rise in her throat as tears gathered in her eyes and spilled down her face. She couldn't remember the last time she cried, and now she was crying in front of a teacher? So embarrassing.

Ms. Aiken said nothing for a moment. She paused and waited for Sharon to let her emotions out. Then, softly, she simply said, 'I'm so glad you shared this with me, and I'm so happy you are here. There's no way I can change what's happened in the past, but I can be here with you now, and maybe we can make the future a little better.' Then Ms. Aiken paused again. She waited. She didn't tell Sharon to move on to her next class. She didn't shoo her out the door. The two of them sat in silence, and somehow, an unspoken agreement was written in the quiet. They would team up to try to create a better future. Sharon would give this school a chance, and she would find herself a home here. The bell for the next class period rang. Ms. Aiken didn't move. Finally, Sharon broke the silence:

'I think I'm going to like it here,' she whispered.

'I think so too. You can stay here as long as you need to this morning. There's plenty of time for you to start your new classes. Just chill with me and settle in,' said Ms. Aiken.

It wasn't easy, and it wasn't instantaneous, but with the help of Ms. Aiken, Sharon did settle in. She found herself getting better grades and making connections with friends, and thankfully, her family stayed in this location until she graduated. Ms. Aiken helped Sharon find a community college where she could take her generals. She transferred to a four-year institution and finished her licensure in special education. After securing her first teaching position, she knew she would be a teacher just like Ms. Aiken.

The first thing Ms. Sharon Robinson hung on the wall of her classroom was a simple home-made poster:

'I See You . . . I Like You . . . I'm Glad You're Here . . . Love, Ms. Robinson.'

Sharon Robinson didn't just experience excellent pedagogy or exemplary case management. Ms. Aiken sat with Sharon in her pain. She didn't tell her not to feel her feelings, but she shared them instead. She opened her heart and offered her time without reservation, and she offered affirmation. Ultimately, Ms. Aiken became a purveyor of hope, and they had a lasting impact on Sharon's life. Empathy and unconditional acceptance are two of the most powerful practices we can choose to implement as special education teachers. The impact of these approaches can make a world of positive difference for students.

Every single student in your class or on your caseload is your responsibility. It's your job to build a relationship with all of them, and it isn't optional. You will receive a list of names at the start of the school year. Every name on the list represents a unique human being who will bring a valuable personal history to your classroom. Some will arrive with all the tools and skills and support necessary to succeed with relative ease. Some will arrive with lots of baggage. which may present a difficulty, until you help them unpack and settle in. Some may carry negative past experiences with teachers. Others may have a bias against the importance of school. It just won't matter that much to them. Still others may have lots of outside stressors which create a challenge, such as addiction in the family, financial instability, or a whole plethora of other unseen obstacles which we couldn't even imagine.

As a special education teacher, your students will have disabilities of a varying nature and extent. Your job is to see the person, not the disability, and to help them prepare for a full, rich life in which they can make a positive contribution to the world and realize their full potential. Educational researcher Dr. Zaretta Hammond defines culturally responsive teaching as

> Your job is to see the person, not the disability, and to help them prepare for a full, rich life in which they can make a positive contribution to the world and realize their full potential.

> an educator's ability to recognize students' cultural displays of learning and meaning making and respond positively and constructively with teaching moves that use cultural knowledge as a scaffold to connect what the student knows to new concepts and content in order to promote effective information processing.
>
> (2015, p. 15)

Essentially, we see who students are and the unique history we bring to the classroom. Then, we craft our instruction to build on each student's unique background.

Why does culturally responsive teaching matter, and how can it help sustain you in your work? Culturally responsive teaching is an imperative in the special education classroom, and it can result in a more enjoyable experience for both you and your students. This chapter offers practical strategies to promote equitable opportunities for all learners, as well as activities you and your students can complete to share their personal histories, deepen relationships, and create a positive and inclusive space for learning. This chapter seeks to answer questions such as the following:

◆ How might you practice unconditional acceptance of every learner, and why is this particularly important for students in special education?

◆ What is a personal history, and why does it matter in special education? How do student histories coincide to create rich learning environments?

◆ How can the tools of culturally responsive teaching bring life to your practice and foster longevity in the profession?

◆ How can we focus on the student, not the label, in order to truly see our students and support their learning?

◆ How can you invite students to share who they are more readily at school? Why does this matter?

◆ What is the role of empathy in effective lesson planning and instruction in special education, and how can it help you?

Unconditional Acceptance

Let me begin with a bit of honesty—not every student will love you, and you will not naturally love every student. At least not at first. This is completely and totally okay. It's natural. It's normal. It's called life. When you find yourself butting heads with a student or struggling to connect, this is a chance to explore creative ways to open your heart a little bit more to find that place of love and acceptance. Ask yourself the right questions, like, 'Why is this difficult for me?' and 'What is actually bothering me about this situation?' **Humans learn and grow from each other, and we can use those difficult relationships as a chance at introspection.**

> Humans learn and grow from each other, and we can use those difficult relationships as a chance at introspection.

If every student was our instant best friend and it was always sunshine, rainbows, and butterflies, we would never have to grow as teachers. Embrace the struggle, and know that once you break down a student's walls and earn their trust, you might create life-saving relationships. Chances are, you aren't the first teacher to have struggled with this particular student. You have the chance to be the teacher who breaks through, and that is a gift! I suggest you commit to the premise of unconditional acceptance of all learners. This means that no matter what, you will accept the student just as they walk through the door, exactly as they are. This doesn't mean you accept undesirable behavior, but you accept the person as a valuable individual who deserves your kind attention.

In practicing unconditional acceptance, love and grace are the name of the game. This doesn't mean we let everyone run wild, willy-nilly, into complete chaos. We can set the stage for improvement in any relationship by maintaining love, assuming that students are doing the best they can with what they have and upholding our expectations. You will find a way to be kind yet firm. When I think back over my teaching career, the students who stand out the most are those who gave me a run for my money at first! They pushed every button they could find and put me to the test to see how I would respond. Once they discovered that I would remain steady, strong, caring, and kind, they moved into a place of trust, and the relationships flourished. For many of them, their entire school experience improved. Teacher Tool 31 offers an activity titled Unconditional Acceptance Reflection to help you put this powerful approach into practice.

Student Personal Histories

As we strive to be culturally inclusive and accept all learners, it is important to remember that each student possesses a unique personal history which shapes who they are and how they see the world. This is true for every single student we work with. Cultural influence begins with our earliest interactions as human beings and creates the lens through which we see the world. This means our students may see things very differently than we do, and this is okay! We can serve them best when we learn and welcome their stories in the school setting. When we provide avenues for them to share the way they see the world and the stories which have shaped who they are, we tell students that we value them and that they matter to us.

Teacher Tool 31: Unconditional Acceptance Reflection

Use this form to reflect on how you might practice unconditional acceptance of who your students are while holding them to standards of the classroom.

Practicing unconditional acceptance:	
Three things I can easily accept from my students: 1. 2. 3.	Three things I struggle to accept from my students: 1. 2. 3.
Potential benefits of unconditional acceptance:	
Three benefits students may enjoy when I practice unconditional acceptance: 1. 2. 3.	Three ways unconditional acceptance may help me enjoy my practice: 1. 2. 3.
Strategies to practice unconditional acceptance:	
Three strategies I may use to remind myself to practice unconditional acceptance include: 1. 2. 3.	

> When we provide avenues for students to share the way they see the world and the stories which have shaped who they are, we tell students that we value them and that they matter to us.

When we see students as unique individuals with rich stories to share, they learn that their importance and potential are not defined by a label on an Individual Education Plan, a set of test scores in a computerized database, or a list of letter grades on a transcript. They are human participants in their own lives poised to accomplish great things and realize their full potential with the support of a teacher who truly cares about them. Sure, we have a file of information on our students in the world of special education, but students are so much more than the information we read in these documents. Too often, the file will tell the story of the deficits rather than the strengths. It will leave out the rich and meaningful memories which have shaped who our students are. I usually read the file with the expectation that it won't give me the full story. I get to discover the magic in each student as I build a relationship with them in real live practice. The negative information in a pile of paperwork will not bias me to expect anything but the best from my students!

There are many strategies you may employ to bring the personal history of each student into your practice. Teacher Tool 32, My Life Map, offers a structured activity students may complete to share key information about their lives. Teacher Tool 33, Who I Am, involves instructions for students to compose poetry which shares about their personal cultural experiences. You can complete these activities along with students to deepen connections.

Line drawing of the student's key life events. This includes her birthplace in Africa, adoption at age 2.5 to America, the schools she has attended, and her favorite sport, soccer. The drawings are ordered 'birth' to 'today.' They are arranged in a flowchart format to create the life map.

Labels Are for Soup Cans

Our students come to us with a special education identification because this is required in order for them to qualify for services.

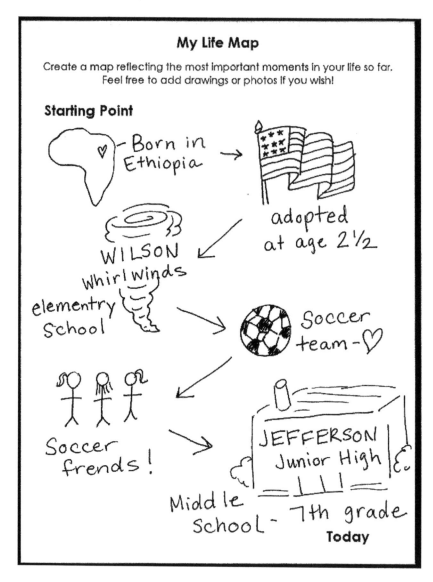

FIGURE 7.1
My Life Map Example Completed by Samri Jorgensen, the Author's Daughter
(Jorgensen, 2022)

Teacher Tool 32: My Life Map

Create a map reflecting the most important moments in your life so far. Feel free to add drawings or photos.

Starting Point

Today

Teacher Tool 33: Who I Am

Name: _____ Date: _____

Brainstorm Ideas:
Complete this chart with memories from your childhood or life:

Smells from your childhood	Places in your home or neighborhood	Close family members
Lands and places your family is from or visits	Sayings in your family	Songs or stories your family sings or tells
Special memories	Tastes from your childhood	Things which were important to you

Create your Poem:
Finish each line with an item from the chart to create your 'I Am From' poem.

I am

_____,

I am

_____,

I am

_____,

I am

_____,

I am

_____,

To be completely forthright, this is a label. Over my years in special education, I have learned that the label assigned to a student says nothing about who they are. Each learner is unique, significant, and possesses their own strengths along with their needs. I believe that labels are for soup cans at the grocery store. In special education, they are nothing but a ticket in the door which allows a student to receive the help and support which can help them thrive. Once we begin our work with them, it is up to us to learn about their positive qualities, perspectives, interests, hopes, and dreams. Essentially, we must learn who they are.

Too often, students are aware of the labels the outside world has put on them. We all endure the pain of being stereotyped, and this is a part of the human experience. The pain of unfair bias can be even more acute for students in special education as they have often experienced stigmatization because of their challenges. We must help students learn that they are so much more than a label or a stereotype assigned to them by the outside world. They have an invaluable core identity made up of positive qualities, even if they don't believe this or the good stuff is hard to find.

> We must help students learn that they are so much more than a label or a stereotype assigned to them by the outside world.

We can help students realize that their personal identity is multifaceted and complex. They are respectable, unique individuals who can decide who they want to be despite any negative messages they have received from others. Teacher Tool 34, My True Identity, offers students the chance to describe who they are as compared to who the outside world has told them to be. Again, you may also complete this activity along with students in order to connect on a deeper level and build relationships.

The Empathy Check

One of the easiest things we can do for our students is to pay attention. Notice the haircuts, the new shoes, the book a kid is reading, the doodle on a notebook. Mentioning the little things you notice in a discreet way can create moments of

Teacher Tool 34: My True Identity

Fill in the outside circle with words others have used to describe you in your life (positive or negative). Fill in the inside circle with words you would use to describe yourself (positive words only!). Realize that the inner circle is who you truly are!

Word Idea Bank:

Kind	Strong	Resilient	Caring	Assertive
Reliable	Honest	Responsible	Loyal	Mature
Creative	Consistent	Appreciative	Capable	Sensitive
Perceptive	Patient	Thoughtful	Trustworthy	Motivated
Funny	Realistic	Serious	Supportive	Friendly

Words others have used to describe me . . .	Words I would use to describe me . . .

MY TRUE IDENTITY . . .

I am:

connection, which mean so much to students. It says, 'I see you, I like you, and I'm glad you are here.' If every kid in your classroom or on your caseload is receiving this message, you are setting the stage for them to succeed. Your classroom becomes a family space where students are completely comfortable, and their relaxed brains are ready to absorb new skills and content. It's a beautiful thing, and it's easier to accomplish than we realize.

The importance of empathy is woven throughout this book, just as empathy ought to be woven throughout teaching practice in special education. The more we can put ourselves in our students' shoes, seeing the world out of their eyes, the better we can create a school experience which works for them. This approach is at the heart of culturally responsive practice as we work to fully understand and embrace our students for all that they are. I believe that the most effective instruction starts with empathy as well. We must plan our lessons in a way that ushers students into engagement, and seeing the learning experience through their lens can help us do just that!

> I see you, I like you, and I'm glad you are here.

I have developed a step-by-step practice called the Empathy Check to set the stage for increased student engagement and learning. The goal is to create lessons which work and which allow students to achieve desired outcomes. When students are set up for success, we can relax and enjoy a less-stressful experience in leading activities and supporting achievement. Table 7.1 details the steps in the Empathy Check process with examples from special education. Teacher Tool 35 offers an Empathy Check Reflection you may use to evaluate a lesson or practice.

Conclusion

I beg of you, check your biases at the door. In order to leave them in the dust, you have to know that they are there. Do the work to recognize the stereotypes and generalizations you may have grown up with and develop an awareness. Denial serves no one. Once you identify your own potential biases, challenge them and refute them in your mind. Then, commit to practice unconditional acceptance of each and every student, each and every

TABLE 7.1 The Empathy Check With Examples.

Steps in the Empathy Check	Examples in Special Education
Gather all materials for a lesson, learning activity, or unit you are preparing to teach.	A special education teacher plans a lesson on sentence writing for fifth grade small group instruction.
Reflect on all student materials. What are the literacy demands students will face? How much will they need to read and interpret directions? Could written information be more concise?	Students will need to be able to read words and phrases in order to build them into sentences. The directions explain this in writing, but verbal directions would help. The special education teacher adds video directions for remote learners and plans to explain this verbally to in-person students.
Reflect on the level of visual support throughout the lesson and included in student materials. Could additional images support clarity?	Some students will be able to manage reading the words. Others may benefit from symbol cues to help them with decoding. The special education teacher adds graphics for support.
Reflect on the clarity of the directions. Sitting in your student's shoes, would these make sense? Are they thorough? Consider completing directions yourself to ensure that they flow and accomplish learning goals.	A few examples would really help make things clear and reduce confusion. The special education teacher plans to model the sentence-building process for all students, or if a student volunteers, a student could model this with prompts as needed.
Reflect on implicit messages students may receive in the lesson materials or assignments. Do they reflect and include all learners?	The sentences are generic and don't really reflect the students. The special education teacher adjusts the lesson to reflect student names and interests from within the group.
Imagine that you are a struggling learner. Where could differentiation help you? Could you benefit from a shortened task or a graphic organizer?	The special education teacher adds visual cues which will help learners who struggle with decoding. Some learners will use a structured sheet to help them organize their sentences on the page.
Consider the student experience of the lesson as a whole. Is there too much prolonged listening? Too much inactive sitting? Where can you add novelty, fun, and interests?	The special education teacher plans to keep the explanation as short as possible and use students to model and share. Student voices are more engaging than the teacher's voice. The lesson involves hands-on activity, so this will take up most of the time.

Teacher Tool 35: Empathy Check Reflection

Use this form to analyze a lesson or unit to ensure empathetic practice.

Step in the Empathy Check	Reflective Analysis
LITERACY DEMANDS: What will my students need to read? Will they be able to decode this? Can they manage the comprehension demands?	
VISUAL SUPPORTS: Describe the visual support included in the lesson including graphics and video. Could additional visuals support understanding?	
DIRECTIONS FOR INDEPENDENT TASKS: Sitting in your student's shoes, would these make sense? Are they thorough? Check for all needed steps.	
IMPLIED MESSAGES: Do the materials reflect and include all learners? What hidden messages may students receive?	
DIFFERENTIATION: Where could differentiation help struggling learners? How could learning tasks be adapted if necessary?	
OVERALL ANALYSIS: Consider the student experience of the lesson as a whole. How might the lesson encourage engagement? Could the lesson be more fun?	

day. Become a researcher of each student and get to know them as individuals, leaving behind any propensity to judge a book by its cover. Ask questions and then listen. Invite them to share their stories in various ways using the tools in this chapter.

Help students understand that their true identity is something they can define based on their many strengths. It has nothing to do with any label anyone else has put on them or any negative message they have received from an external source. Each day is a new day for them to create the person they want to be. It's a beautiful journey, and we get to be on it with our students! Keep in mind that the better we know and understand our students, the more we can use this knowledge to drive our instructional decisions. Empathy is the missing instructional link which will help us truly meet their needs. So I implore you, embrace your students with all their quirks and needs, and focus on the amazing personal history and strengths they bring to your practice!

Simple Snapshot

+ Unconditional acceptance means embracing students exactly as they are.
+ Learning about student personal histories helps us serve them better.
+ Labels are nothing more than a ticket in the door. Each student is unique.
+ Helping students define their true identity is a powerful positive practice.
+ Running instructions through the Empathy Check ensures utmost effectiveness.

Reflection Questions

Use the following questions to reflect on what you have learned in the chapter. You may choose to journal about them or discuss them with a partner or small group to gain further insights.

1. What is your perspective on the concept of 'unconditional acceptance'? How might this approach help you as a teacher? How may this be difficult?
2. What are some practices you use to invite students to share their personal histories in your practice? How might you bring out who they are even more?

3. Where do you find the most common ground with your students? Where do you find the most differences?
4. What are your thoughts on the concept that 'labels are for soup cans'? How might you apply this idea in your work?
5. How might the Empathy Check support you in making your lessons more culturally inclusive? What are your thoughts on this tool?
6. What is your overall philosophy of education with regards to inclusion for all students? How does this help you, and where do you find challenges?

References

Hammond, Zaretta. (2015). *Culturally Responsive Teaching and the Brain*. Thousand Oaks, CA: Corwin Press.

Jorgensen, Samri. (2022). *My Life Map* [line drawing]. Anoka Middle School for the Arts, Anoka, MN.

8

Connecting With Families

Mr. Cho knew he wasn't supposed to have a favorite student, but one of the sixth graders on his special education caseload, DJ, was really standing out. DJ was funny, creative, and high energy. DJ kept Mr. Cho on his toes every day, and that was turning out to be a good thing. They somehow shared the same sense of humor, and laughing through the day was helping DJ manage his needs in the areas of anger management and following school rules. Mr. Cho made sure to divide his time wisely among his students, but he had to admit that his daily interactions with DJ were a highlight of his day. He made sure to make a connection of some kind with DJ's mom, Graciela, at least once a week with positive information, whether it was a phone call or a note home. DJ and Graciela both loved this, and it kept DJ's negative behaviors at bay. When there was a blip, which did happen here and there, it was much easier for Mr. Cho to solve problems with Graciela because they already knew each other so well.

Near the end of the school year, it was time for DJ's Individual Education Planning meeting. This required annual meeting had been something Graciela absolutely dreaded. Basically, she had to sit around a table and hear about everything that was wrong with her kid. She always left the meetings feeling downtrodden and overwhelmed. Questions would ruminate in her mind: 'Do these teachers blame me for my son's issues? Do they think I'm a crappy parent? Am I a crappy parent?' She had to keep her head held high and move on, but going to

DOI: 10.4324/9781003322528-9

the meetings usually felt like a trip to the dentist to have a tooth pulled. She hoped things would be different this year. She liked Mr. Cho and felt comfortable when she talked to him.

The day of the meeting arrived, and the team gathered around the table. DJ decided to hang out in the classroom next door and said he would come into the meeting if he felt like it. DJ's mom, Graciela, dumped some Legos out of her purse to keep him occupied before heading over to join the team.

Mr. Cho started the meeting:

'It's pretty cool that you carry Legos in your purse. DJ sure loves Legos!'

'Ha, yeah, I have to admit I never expected I'd have a purse full of Legos always at my side when I became a mom,' she replied.

The team laughed. The ice was broken. The meeting felt positive and comfortable from there. Mr. Cho kept things concise and ran the meeting like a conversation. It wasn't a litany of negatives, and he asked each team member to start by talking about DJ's strengths. Over the course of the meeting, Graciela said something that Mr. Cho would never forget, and it stuck with him for the rest of his teaching career.

'DJ is being successful this year,' she said, 'because this is the first time a teacher has liked him.'

WHOA. Mr. Cho was blown away. Who wouldn't like DJ? He was the best! Sure, he struggled with anger and behavior, but overall he was simply awesome!

Mr. Cho said just that. After a long pause, Graciela asked for a tissue. Years of frustration with the school system were melting off her back, and she softly shed a few tears of relief. Mr. Cho went on to describe the strengths he had observed in DJ and laid out ideas for his educational programming. He offered Graciela choices and incorporated DJ's perspective by ushering him into the meeting and asking him questions to gain his input. Graciela's preferences combined with what DJ offered drove all team decisions. All participants walked away with a clear plan for DJ's continuing success, and Graciela left with the sense that her son was in good hands. She believed in a bright future for her son and had a new hope and trust in the school system.

After the meeting, Mr. Cho reflected on the conversation. He resolved to ALWAYS find a way to connect with parents as an ally. His main message would be 'I really like your kid, and I want them to succeed!' With this at the forefront, everything else would fall into place.

Mr. Cho's story illustrates the ideal situation for a special education teacher. He achieved a positive connection with Graciela and became a source of strength and hope for both the student and the parent. Relationships with parents are a pivotal part of our work in special education. They can be a source of great joy and information-sharing, or they can be a source of struggle and stress. Making sure our relationships with parents/guardians are as positive as possible can help us tremendously in our work!

There is a scene in my life which I will never, ever forget. It is the day I took my brand-new baby home from the hospital. When I left the house, I was not a mom. When I returned, not only had I become a mom, I held a tiny little life in my hands. And the tiny little life was screaming and needed a diaper change. It was amazing, beautiful, incredible, and terrifying all at the same time. It was more responsibility than I had ever experienced in my life. In my hands I held so many hopes, dreams, and aspirations for this little one. I wanted to get it right and be a fantastic mom. I melted with love for this child, and I wanted to protect him from all the evils in the world. More than anything else, I wanted him to grow up into someone happy.

The other day I will never forget is the day I met my daughter in an Ethiopian orphanage. She sat in the corner with a blank stare on her face. She had lost everything, she was in deep pain, and she wasn't even two years old yet. When I held her, I melted again. I wanted to love her so hard that I healed her hurts and brought her back to life. It took time, but she settled into American family life quickly and became a joyful, free, peaceful young lady. She flourished. Again, when I watched her toddling around in the backyard, I was filled with hope that she would grow into a happy person. The same hopes, dreams, and aspirations flooded me. It's the deepest and truest love I have ever experienced.

> Every student on your caseload or class list is somebody's baby.

My own children have reminded me of a critical fact which drives my work with families: every student on your caseload or class list is somebody's baby. Each of them have their own story. Some of these stories involve loads of love and resources. Some of these stories involve pain and scarcity. Either way, at some point, that student was held in someone's arms and (hopefully) treasured. We do best to assume that parents/guardians are doing the very best they can with the reserves of love and resources they have. There is no ultimate 'right way' to be a parent, and everyone goes about it in their own way as dictated by their own upbringing, culture, beliefs, and values. This is a beautiful thing. We aren't robots, and it's all part of the lovely diversity in the human condition. The families we work with are navigating the added complexity involved in parenting a child with a disability.

As special education teachers, we spend about 7.5 hours with our students each day. We find them delightful, enjoyable, and sometimes, we find them challenging. It's a simple truth that many of our students demand a lot of energy, vigilance, and support, and no matter how much we love them, sometimes we get tired. Now imagine that you are serving these students 24 hours a day, 7 days a week, 365 days a year. Add to this the fact that you know the best approaches to the student, but some don't agree with the way you choose to care for them. For some icing on the cake, throw on legally required meetings, doctor's appointments, managing medications, and the list goes on. Our parents/guardians are champions. Each is bearing the brunt of the responsibility for helping their child become a happy, healthy part of society, no matter what that looks like.

So if you remember one thing from this chapter, please make it this: check your judgments at the door. Judging parents, complaining about parents, and blaming parents can be rampant among teachers. This serves no one. It's unjust, it's not nice, it's a big-time no-no, and it hurts collaboration. Parents need our love just as much as our students do. We are all in this together! We have the chance to encourage parents and help give them hope, or we can give them a headache. It all comes down to how we build connections. This chapter will explore questions such as the following:

◆ How might you open lines of communication to tap into the rich resource of knowledge parents/guardians possess regarding the student's strengths and needs?

- ◆ How might you use information you gain from parents/ guardians to best help your students?
- ◆ What are some approaches you may use to build trust to bring comfort and love to parents?
- ◆ How might you best communicate best with families?
- ◆ What might be some strategies to maintain a focus on shared goals and build the sense that everyone is working for the same outcomes?

Asking the Right Questions

> As special education teachers, it is our job to find the magic to unlock the right approaches to make schoolwork for the student. Often, parents and guardians are already holding the key, and we must build a bridge so they trust us enough to share it.

Nobody knows a student better than their parent/guardian. They are the experts on the student. Most of the time, they have been there much longer than you have. Perhaps there has been pain and difficulty along the way. Parents have an unspoken record of details about their child which can provide the keys to success at school. As special education teachers, it is our job to find the magic to unlock the right approaches to make schoolwork for the student. Often, parents and guardians are already holding the key, and we must build a bridge so they trust us enough to share it. We do this by offering warmth, kindness, and connection, which invites them to open the gates of information.

So what might this actually look like? Well, to be proactive, it means getting to know as many parents as quickly as possible. Once you make the initial connection, it's time to start asking the right questions to invite parents to share. The best questions are open-ended in nature to get parents talking and open communication. Too often, we fall into the habit of asking 'yes or no' questions, which fail to get parents/guardians talking. For example, rather than asking 'What are some of your child's strengths?' we may ask 'Does he like sports?' The second question narrows the potential responses and leads the parent/guardian toward a simple, one-word answer.

We are wise to craft questions which invite elaborative responses. I call these invitational questions. Two helpful stems which lead to open communication include 'What are some . . .' and 'How might . . .' For example, special education teachers may ask, 'What are some of your student's interests?' or 'How might I best help your student with managing their emotions?' Teacher Tool 36 offers an activity titled Crafting Invitational Questions, which offers you the chance to develop open-ended questions which may help open the lines of communication with parents and guardians.

Gathering the Right Information

> Don't interrogate the parents with rapid-fire questions but ask open-ended questions to get the parent talking and then listen carefully to what they share.

The first thing I recommend you do when there is even the faintest hint of an issue with a student is to become a researcher. Remember that students are constantly communicating to you with their behavior and sending you messages about how to 'make things work' for them in your classroom. Reflect on everything you've observed at school as a starting point. Then, dig a little deeper and find out as much as you can about the student's situation outside of school. Give the family a call not to tell on the student or report anything negative, but simply to initiate a connection and gather information. Don't interrogate the parents with rapid-fire questions but ask open-ended questions to get the parent talking and then listen carefully to what they share. I promise you that there is helpful information waiting for you which will prevent bigger issues and ultimately help the student out!

Keep track of the key learnings you glean from your conversations with parents. In my practice, I have learned that writing everything down is very helpful. Just like students, parents/guardians notice when we remember information they share with us about their lives and their children. It can bolster relationships to keep careful track of what we learn from them and mention these elements from time to time. Teacher Tool 37 offers a form titled What Do I Know? which provides a space for you to keep a record of what you have learned about each of

Teacher Tool 36: Crafting Invitational Questions

Parents/guardians are our best resources to help us learn as much as possible about our students. Use this form to craft open-ended questions to get parents talking about various key areas. Remember that 'What are some' and 'How might' are excellent sentence-starters for invitational questions which get people talking.

Area: Social Functioning	
What are some . . .?	How might I . . .?

Area: Emotional Functioning	
What are some . . .?	How might I . . .?

Area: Behavioral Functioning	
What are some . . .?	How might I . . .?

Area: Academic Functioning	
What are some . . .?	How might I . . .?

Area: General Information	
What are some . . .?	How might I . . .?

Teacher Tool 37: What Do I Know?

When a student is experiencing difficulty with any area of functioning in the school setting, it can be helpful to learn as much as you can about the parent/guardians' perspective. Use this form to compile all of the information you know about the student's needs, preferences, and interests.

Area: Social Functioning	
Strengths and needs:	What does this mean for my work with the student?

Area: Emotional Functioning	
Strengths and needs:	What does this mean for my work with the student?

Area: Behavioral Functioning	
Strengths and needs:	What does this mean for my work with the student?

Area: Academic Functioning	
Strengths and needs:	What does this mean for my work with the student?

Area: General Information	
Strengths and needs:	What does this mean for my work with the student?

your students. Keeping this handy when making contact with parents can help you build your knowledge base to best meet student needs.

Allyship and Shared Goals

For many families, school is the place where they are learning a lot about their child, and this can be a good thing or a challenge. Parents/guardians send their little ones to school with hopes that academics will come easily, that social skills will blossom, that behavior will be a piece of cake, and that their student will eventually graduate with honors. Obviously, it rarely fully pans out this way, and parents are on a journey of understanding and accepting how school will 'work' for their kiddo. Over my years in education, I have had to support parents through some difficult realizations. For some, the future they dreamed of for their child turns out vastly different from their initial aspirations. Acceptance takes time, and it can involve some difficult emotions. It can look like grieving a loss, including feelings such as denial, pain, guilt, anger, and sadness. In these situations, I have tried to be an empathetic listener and a supportive presence.

> We can help parents/guardians understand that we all have the same goals, that we all want the best for the student, and that we all have helpful roles to play in this process.

We can help parents/guardians understand that we all have the same goals, that we all want the best for the student, and that we all have helpful roles to play in this process. As mentioned earlier, we open the lines of communication with invitational questions. We build relationships with parents/guardians just as we do with our students. We can also invite deeper and more detailed information sharing through the use of surveys. Teacher Tool 38 provides a parent survey which can support open communication and offer you a rich resource to support students. This may be converted into an online form or could be sent home and returned.

Teacher Tool 38: Parent Survey

I am so excited to work with your student! Please complete the following to help me understand your perspective and best meet the needs of your student at school. THANK YOU for taking the time to share this information! We are all in this together.

What should I know about your student?	
Strengths:	Concern areas:

What strategies are most helpful for your student?

What makes your student most happy?	
At home:	At school:

What makes your student upset?	
At home:	At school:

What else should I know about your student or your family?

Be Kind, Be Humble, Be Real

In the age of technology, there are so many ways to communicate with parents/guardians. As a parent myself, I have connected with my children's teachers through phone, email, virtual meetings, apps they ask me to download on my phone, and of course, the classic face-to-face conference. As a special education teacher, I have utilized most of these approaches myself with the addition of translating written documents for families and using the services of an interpreter as needed to ensure clear messages. What is the best mode of conveying messages with families? Whichever fits the preferences and needs of the parent/guardian.

> What is the best mode of conveying messages with families? Whichever fits the preferences and needs of the parent/guardian.

The best way to discover this is simple—ASK! Early in the school year, ask parents whether they prefer a phone call or an email and which language they prefer. In the past I was composing lengthy emails only to learn that the recipient didn't have the personal resources to comprehend the information in this medium. This parent needed phone calls, and thus, this is what I provided. I kept our conversations brief and checked in often, and it worked out great! It is entirely okay to set a time limit for a phone call at the outset of the conversation with a statement such as, 'I just want to check in, and I have about ten minutes.' This sets the stage for a focused conversation, which makes best use of the time.

Electronic communication allows us to send quick messages without knowledge of exactly when the information will be received by the parent. While it may be convenient, we may be wiser to make a phone call if we need to be certain parents receive our messages right away. Again, it all depends on the specific needs of the family. Teacher Tool 39 offers a communication plan special education teachers may use to identify the optimal methods for reaching specific student families.

Teacher Tool 39: Communication Plan for Parents, Guardians, and Families

Complete this form to develop a plan for communication with each family. This form may be particularly useful to organize parent requests and ensure follow-through on action steps. It also offers the chance to plan the frequency and modalities you will utilize for communication. Reproduce this form as needed to plan for each family on your caseload or receiving your services.

Student Name: _____ Grade: _____ Parent/Guardian Name(s): _____	
Family Description: (List unique strengths, needs and requests)	
Preferred Mode of Communication:	**Priority Topics for Communication:**
Timeline and frequency of interaction:	
Questions this family has asked:	**Resources this family needs:**

Navigating Challenges

Parenting is not easy. Kids don't come with an instruction manual or a handbook to tell you what to do. Being a mom has been one of the most challenging and anxiety-producing experiences of my life. Why? Because I love my children so deeply, and I want what's best for them so much! We can either add to the stress of parenting for our families or help to alleviate it. When negative situations arise, the most helpful special education teachers come alongside parents and return to the question, How can we solve this together? (Leenders et al., 2019). Starting with this question, we can move forward with the conversation. When times get tough and we have negative information to share, we can fall back on the preexisting positive relationship we have built with the family. We can start with the premise that parents have positive intent and that they are doing the best they can with what they have.

> Whenever we must share something negative with a parent or guardian, we do well to start with empathy.

Whenever we must share something negative with a parent or guardian, we do well to start with empathy. If I was receiving this phone call, how would I want to hear the message? If I was reading the email, what would I want it to say? Then, we begin with something positive. I never start a conversation with something negative, no matter how tired or frustrated I may feel. There is always something good to share with the family. After sharing the negative information, I also try to end with a hopeful message, which is future-focused. I say that I believe in the student and that we will all move forward together in a positive direction. And most importantly, I believe it!

We can be proactive and solve problems before they start by setting up clear roles and responsibilities between students, parents/guardians, and ourselves as special education teachers. When we make this clear, we help parents know exactly what to expect. Teacher Tool 40 provides an activity titled Student-Parent-Teacher Commitments, which all parties may sign to express agreement. You may also choose to create your own version of this document specific to your practice and meeting the needs of families.

Teacher Tool 40: Student-Parent-Teacher Commitments

Student Commitments:

- I will come to school every day well rested and on time and remain in school until dismissal.
- I will come to school with necessary materials and prepared to work.
- I will complete all assignments on time.
- I will ask for help or assignments missed when needed.
- I will respect the rights of others at all times.

Parent/Guardian Commitments:

- I will make sure my child is well rested and at school on time and remains in school until dismissal.
- I will make sure my child is prepared with the necessary materials and ready to learn.
- I will communicate any concerns with my child's case manager and/or teacher.
- I will read, sign, and return progress reports and teacher communications and attend conferences/meetings as requested.

Teacher Commitments:

- I will ensure that the Individual Education Plan takes place.
- I will provide a classroom environment conducive to learning.
- I will communicate my expectations, instructional goals, and grading system with parents through conferences, progress reports, e-mails, or by telephone.
- I will provide students who have been absent with missed assignments.
- I will accept and respect the cultural differences of my students.
- I will do whatever it takes to see students make progress on their goals.
- I will respond to requests thoroughly and as soon as possible.

Signatures:

X_____   X_____   X_____

Student   Parent/Guardian(s)   Special Education Teacher

Conclusion

Be a kind, considerate communicator in all endeavors involving parents/guardians. This seems as if it should be a no-brainer, but too often it is not. Think about how your actions impact other people, and always shoot for the goal of consistent kindness. Connections with families matter much more than you think! Parents are the first experts on their children, and they are also the source of initial programming for each and every child. Get to know parents and build a relationship, and you will find that you and your students benefit greatly. The better you get to know the student's family situation, the better you can understand their needs and strive to meet them. Find ways to invite parents to share, and keep a careful record of what you learn from them.

See every adult stakeholder in the child's life as an equal and an ally, offering a rich resource on how you can be a better teacher for the student. Building bridges instead of fences will benefit everyone. Parents need us to practice empathy to the greatest extent that we can. It can be hard to put ourselves in their shoes, but doing so will create a foundation for connections which greatly benefit students. Select communication methods which work best for families, and make sure you meet their unique needs. Start and end all conversations with positivity, and develop shared commitments for effective collaboration. Remember that you all share the same goal: the success of the student, and you are all in this together!

Simple Snapshot

- ◆ Parents/guardians are the most valuable resource we have as case managers.
- ◆ Asking invitational questions can initiate strong, positive relationships.
- ◆ We can reduce our stress by seeing parents/guardians as allies with the same goals.
- ◆ Utilize the preferred method of communication for each family.

- Start with positive information and end with positive information, always.
- Invite parents/guardians to develop shared commitments to support their child.

Reflection Questions

Use the following questions to reflect on what you have learned in the chapter. You may choose to journal about them or discuss them with a partner or small group to gain further insights.

1. What are some strategies you have tried to get to know families? How might the approaches from this chapter help you try new practices?
2. What are some of the questions you like to use to help get parents sharing? How might the invitational sentence stems help you?
3. How might the parent survey prove useful in your practice? What questions might you take away or add?
4. Which modes of communication do you prefer in your practice (email, phone calls, online meetings, etc.). How might you select the best plan for communicating with families?
5. What are your thoughts on setting up shared commitments between parents/guardians, students, and teachers? How might this help you?
6. How do you navigate challenging situations involving parents/guardians?

Reference

Leenders, H., de Long, J., Monfrance, M., & Haelermands, C. (2019). Building strong parent-teacher relationships in primary education: The challenge of two-way communication. *Cambridge Journal of Education*, vol. 49, no. 4, pp. 519–33, https://doi.org/10.1080/0305 764X.2019.1566442.

9

The Classroom Management Adventure

As a fifth-grade special education teacher, Ms. Walters taught small groups to help students with needs related to their diagnosis of autism spectrum disorder. All the students were brilliant, fun, and creative, but many struggled with their social skills and their ability to connect with others. Some of them also struggled with sensory issues and became overstimulated and upset at loud noises. Within the group there was a young girl who was a bit of an outlier, AJ. She had a big, huge personality, and you always knew when AJ was in the room. She loved to communicate and would talk at length about her area of special interest: cats. AJ knew the history of the domestic housecat back to the days of ancient Egypt. She knew every species of cat in the wild kingdom. She was a walking cat encyclopedia, and the trouble was, sometimes people didn't want to learn cat trivia or listen to a lecture on the role of cats in the farmsteads of the early 1800s. AJ had a big, loud voice, a boisterous personality, and an infectious smile.

Being AJ's teacher was an act of daily love and patience. Ms. Walters murmured a quiet reminder to herself whenever AJ entered the room to show love and kindness. AJ's big personality and volume tended to set off the students who struggled with sensory overload. This morning, Ms. Walters was exhausted. She had trouble sleeping the night before, and she was in a cranky mood. Unfortunately, AJ was feeling extra, well, extra and was a nonstop chatterbox.

'AJ, I need you to be quiet today, okay? We have a lot to do,' Ms. Walters said, trying to head AJ off at the pass.

DOI: 10.4324/9781003322528-10

'But I just need to tell you guys one more thing,' requested AJ.

'No. Not today. We're done for today.' Even as it came out of her mouth, Ms. Walters knew it sounded way too harsh, and she spoke it too abrasively.

Sure enough, AJ stood up quickly, so quickly in fact that her chair made a loud flip behind her. AJ raised her voice and released, 'No one ever gives a CRAP about me. I just want to tell you ONE MORE THING!'

'That's it. I can't do this today. Go out in the hallway,' said Ms. Walters.

From here, AJ dissolved into tears. Loud, wailing tears, sprinkled with complaints and a few choice words of sorrow and frustration. The rest of the group began to follow suit, and tears could be seen glowing in the eyes of the other students as they felt the stress of the moment.

'Oh gosh, what have I done,' thought Ms. Walters. She knew exactly where things could have gone the other way. She could have listened to one more cat fact. She could have invited AJ to tell her after their group. She could have spoken quietly and gently when she gave the redirection. Now, things were escalating, and she had lost the group.

Ms. Walters took a moment to calm herself. She inhaled a slow, deep breath and said to herself, 'This will be okay.' She stepped into the hallway to help AJ while keeping one eye on the other students. AJ continued to cry for a few more minutes, but as Ms. Walters offered a calm presence, AJ became calm too. She rejoined the group. By the time all was said and done, students missed out on about five minutes of instruction, and everything was indeed okay.

Ms. Walters felt humbled by this experience but hopeful that she could take a new approach with AJ with the understanding that none of the undesirable behaviors were purposeful. AJ was doing the best she could to manage the challenges of school. She needed an ally, not an enemy. She completely shifted her thinking about AJ's behaviors and decided instead to see them as messages about what she needed. And what did she need most? Love, patience, and gentle guidance.

The next day AJ bounced into class joyfully, and Ms. Walters met her with a new idea.

'Say, AJ, how about we start and end our group with one cat fact each day. Would you be able to come up with something for us?' Ms. Walters offered.

'Absolutely!' said AJ. 'I got you covered, Ms. Walters!' Creating a structured way for AJ to share about her key interest area worked *perfectly. Ms. Walters continued to view behavior as communication, understanding that when she listened to the unspoken requests of her students, she could proactively meet needs before they became big issues.*

What a day Ms. Walters had! She learned that flexibility, empathy, patience, and innovation are the key to effective classroom management. She also learned that at times, there would be hiccups and missteps. Supporting students with challenging behaviors can be one of the most difficult parts of the job in special education. This area of teaching practice can be highly unpredictable and emotionally charged. It can make or break relationships and lead to a peaceful learning environment or a setting of stressful chaos. So how can you maintain a happy heart in the face of even the most unreasonable, unacceptable, unruly behaviors? Let's dive in and find out!

In the world of special education, we work with some of the most unique, original, different groups of students anyone could ever imagine, and this can be a gift! There is no way to predict the dynamics of our groups. There is no way to imagine how the intricacies of each individual student and their individual strengths and their individual needs and their individual education plans will fit together into the bigger puzzle. Some students go together like peanut butter and jelly. Others combine like gasoline and matches. And our job is to bring them all together, for better or for worse, and to create a situation in which learning can happen. Over my years in the classroom, I have made thousands if not millions of mistakes when it comes to classroom management. I have learned how to get things back on track when issues arise and the group goes off the rails. I have also learned to avoid common mistakes which will create issues among students.

Have you ever gone camping? I mean rustic camping. Like, in a tent. Not a fancy camper, not a glamping trip. You make meticulous preparations, carefully select your footwear, pack your camp meals, and hope for the best. Then, you are at the mercy of Mother Nature. You may experience glorious sunsets, tasty S'mores, relaxing afternoons in a canoe, and comfy nights of fitful sleep. You may encounter thunderstorms, torrential rains, rampant bugs munching on every inch of your body, extreme heat, freezing temperatures, and even—*gasp*—bears. This is kind of the way classroom management plays out in special education. Even the most experienced camper may be unprepared for what is thrown their way. We can prepare for the unexpected, but even more importantly, we have to prepare our hearts and minds to weather whatever challenges may come along.

> No matter what happens, when you know your purpose and you try to see the best in your students, you can keep your sanity and your love for teaching.

For me, it comes down to one thing. As long as I show up every day and love kids, I am good to go. Whatever may come up, I try to see it through the lens of my fondness for each and every individual in the classroom. I try to recognize their behavior as communication. What are they telling me? How can I respond in a way that is most proactive? It all comes down to my mindset. There will be fabulous days in your classroom, and then there will be those days that you find a mouse in your sleeping bag or a spider in your hair (not literally—I circled back to the camping analogy there). No matter what happens, when you know your purpose and you try to see the best in your students, you can keep your sanity and your love for teaching.

My number one offense in the classroom? Talking WAY TOO MUCH. My intentions were pure. I wanted to communicate clearly and make sure students knew exactly what I was talking about. I wanted to give them every opportunity to be successful by giving them all the information. The problem? Just a few sentences in, students weren't listening anymore. When I had the chance to work as an instructional coach and observe hundreds of lessons, I noticed one clear pattern: the most effective classroom managers asked TONS of questions, and they called on everyone. They pulled students in and engaged them by bringing their voices out. The teachers who took up the air time with their own voices were the ones who struggled with undesirable student behavior every time. Asking lots of questions and leaving quiet time for students to think allows them to stick with what you are teaching. Otherwise, they disconnect and get bored or distracted.

When it comes to special education, there is another key reason to keep our verbal communication concise: many students have invisible difficulties with language processing. 'Receptive language' is a fancy word for the skills we use to interpret the words that we hear or read. For many students, extra time is needed for them to kick on those receptive language skills. When I was little miss chat-a-thon early in my career, I was overloading their ears and minds with too many words. I lost them, and they lost me, and the result was often disengagement. **Talk less, listen more, and students will engage!**

Another mistake I often made was relying too heavily on lengthy lists of rules. Over time I learned that every time I gave a student a rule, it was like an invitation for him or her to break it. Does this mean we have anarchy in our classrooms? It becomes a free-for-all? Students swinging from the rafters? No. Of course not. There have to be guidelines. We do best when we build a relationship with students first, even before we give them our 'rules.' Why? Because when we have a positive relationship, our students usually bring their best selves to the classroom, and we don't even need many pre-written rules. Over my time in education, I have learned to boil everything down into two umbrella rules for the classroom, which I call our agreements. They are as follows:

I will learn.

I will let everyone else learn.

Simple as that. Then, through a positive relationship, I help the students engage with each other in a way which will allow the two agreements to happen. Just thought I would toss it out there in case it helps you. I believe that every teacher finds their own way to set students up for success. We've all been told to pick our battles wisely, but I don't even think of them as battles. When there is a situation that needs to be addressed, we approach it together and try to figure it out. I always make a connection to the world outside of school and how building skills to engage in the classroom in a positive way will eventually translate to success at a job in the future. Everything, all the time, is geared toward understanding the student so that I can offer them love and a positive relationship through empathetic practice. Okay, but enough about me. You will find your way to orchestrate even the most high-need group. Believe it! Fear not!

The simple solution? Special education teachers must tend to their own health and wholeness. From this place, they may take on the attitude that no matter what may arise, love for students will prevail. Special educators may commit to view students through the lens of unconditional acceptance. The content of this chapter will explore additional questions related to the classroom management adventure, which includes the following:

- ◆ How might special education teachers prioritize active engagement to mitigate undesirable student behavior?
- ◆ What are some strategies you can use to maintain a healthy mindset concerning student behavior?
- ◆ How might you manage your difficulties without taking student behavior personally?
- ◆ What are some approaches you can use to balance kindness and boundaries in the classroom?
- ◆ How might the idea that 'all behavior is a message' support longevity and effectiveness in special education?
- ◆ What are some strategies you may use to preserve relationships with students even through difficulty?

In any educational setting, some days will be better than others. To return to the camping analogy, there will be days of sunshine and days of torrential rain. No matter what happens, when you strive to see the best in your students every day, you can better maintain their commitment to the rewarding work of special education.

Boredom Begets Behavior

Bored students tend to act out. In fact, I might say that bored humans tend to act out. Our students are energetic, expressive, unique individuals with so much to share, and yet we stifle them all day long in the classroom. Boredom begets disengagement. What might this mean for you? It means busting boredom among students can support you in helping them learn and grow. It means that if you aren't having any fun, they probably aren't either. Most importantly, it means that you will like your job better when you can infuse your classroom with fun, novelty, and high-interest content.

How can you tell if your students are engaging? I suggest that you hook in your big fish. Let's return to the camping analogy. If you've ever gone camping, you may have been next to a lake or pond. Perhaps you went fishing. Chances are, you were hoping to hook a nice, big fish that you could show off to all your friends. One that you could pose with in a photo for your social media, proving to everyone that you have fishing prowess. You probably weren't too interested in pulling in a little baby guppy. What's my point? There is a connection. Trust me.

You might think of your classroom as your own little pond. In this rich ecosystem, there are the little minnows who tend to stick together and hover around the surface. They don't usually make a lot of waves, and they aren't necessarily your biggest concern. Also living in your pond, you will usually have one or two big-time, boss-of-the-waters fish who can stir up the waters pretty quickly. You could think of these as the leaders in the group. Now, when we think of leadership, we usually think of this as a positive thing. Leaders use their powers for good, not evil. However, this isn't always the case. In your classroom, you will have leaders. Your big fish. They have the power in the pond. When they are having a good day, the group is having a good day. When they are cranky, the class is cranky. As a special education teacher, connecting with these students can make your life run smooth as the surface of a gorgeous fish-filled waterway.

> Make an intentional effort to connect with student leaders as early as you can.

As you start the year with your students, observe them carefully. Who is setting the tone for the room? Who do the other students seem to notice? Who gets the most laughs? Who do they glance at when it's time to follow a direction? These are your big fish. Make an intentional effort to connect with student leaders as early as you can. They are used to commanding the attention of the room, so start this off right for them by offering them positive attention. Notice little things about them, ask them questions about themselves, and convey that you care about their success. Expect to be challenged, but stay consistent. Once students learn that you are there for them, that you are a calm, composed master of the pond and that you truly do care about their success, you will win them over. Now, am I telling you to ignore the rest of the fish who swim in your waters? Of course not. All of them need your attention, care, and support. I am suggesting that it is wise to prioritize a bit because you may find that the entire group warms up to you once you achieve a trusting and mutually respectful relationship with the leaders, or the big fish, among your group.

Once you have your biggest fish on the hook, share the responsibility of making the school world as fun as possible. Invite them to bring their creativity into lessons. Ask them to think of ways to infuse the learning with novelty. Pick their brain on what is going well and what is not, with the overall goal of a productive and fun learning environment. The student will take pride in the fact that you are tapping into his or her leadership, and you will benefit from less stress, less headache, and less pressure to bring the fun all on your own!

The Q-Tip

Mr. Jackson's first year in special education was going well so far. When he first landed the job, he had been a little nervous about working in a special education program for students with significant social, emotional, and behavioral needs in fourth and fifth grade. Would he have the skills to handle it? What if the behaviors were too much? What if a student threw his shoes on the roof? What if a student ran away or climbed up the water tower near the school? His mind created a hundred different scenarios, none of which had come true . . . yet.

*He was pleasantly surprised to discover that the students who were labeled with 'emotional/behavioral disorder' weren't actually so disordered at all. They were **awesome**. Each student was a character with his or her* own unique quirks, and sure, there were challenges at times, but overall, he found them each delightful. His days were not without moments of difficulty, and there were certainly moments when he wasn't sure how to handle the situation, but with the support of his cooperating teacher, he always figured it out. His favorite part about the job was the connections he was building with the students. It was so energizing. In college he had learned that a positive relationship made all the difference, and this was definitely playing out in real life. He could tell the students trusted and respected him, and he loved to use humor to keep class fun. The kids were actually learning and growing. It was working. Yes. Amazing. Yay!

That was until the program got a new student. We'll call him Alex. Alex was a living, breathing roller coaster. At one moment he could be warm, charming, and so much fun. The next, he could hurl insults which were so on target, they stung. Alex had a presence and a command over the other students the minute he walked in. They brought out their worst behavior to impress him, and the next thing Mr. Jackson knew, the whole class had flipped on him. That warm, caring, happy-land class-room community was no more. Instead, he found himself in constant power struggles with Alex. Any limit set down by adults, Alex would push as far as he could or completely ignore. This student was master-fully running the show, and learning had come to a complete halt.

Ms. Jackson was crushed. He had lost his mojo. He felt like the worst teacher in the world and went home each day devastated. At times he questioned whether or not he belonged in this profession. After all the cash he had shelled out for tuition, all the hopes and dreams, was he ready to walk away from being a teacher? Every time he walked in the classroom, Alex had a jab waiting for him. Whether it was his outfit, his haircut, his shoes, the look on his face, Alex could say things that cut to the core and made all the other students laugh. It was soul-crushing, and all the teacher could think was, 'Wow. I'm a terrible teacher. I'm a screwup. I have failed.'

One morning when he arrived at school, he found a single Q-tip on his desk with a sticky note on it. It read, 'Let's chat at lunch,' and was signed by his colleague Ms. Villejo. 'Oh great, she knows I suck at this,' Mr. Jackson thought. He got through the bumpy morning in his usual survival mode. When lunch rolled around, he sat down in the break room with Ms. Villejo ready to try to explain himself for being the worst teacher who ever walked the earth.

'Did you get the Q-tip?' she asked.

'Um . . . yeah . . . ?' he replied with a question in his voice.

'I want you to keep it nearby this school year, and every time you see it, I want you to think about what it stands for,' she explained.

'Okay, thanks! So what does it stand for?' he asked with a chuckle.

'Quit. Taking. It. Personally,' she said. She then went on to explain that in education, students come to us with their own world of pain, hurt, and difficulty, and sometimes they take it out on the safest person around—their teacher. If we take it personally when we have difficulty connecting with a student, we will burn ourselves out. In this conversation, Mr. Jackson realized that the hurtful insults were part of the student's disability, and it did him no good to take them to heart. Applying common sense allowed him to become Teflon-tough against the jabs, seeing through to the underlying unmet needs in the student. It had nothing to do with his teaching abilities, his fashion sense, or his taste in shoes.

Over the next few days, the power struggles stopped. When Mr. Jackson was able to stop taking things personally, he was able to keep a cool head and pick his battles carefully. He didn't respond to the insults and jabs, or he laughed them off. Oddly enough, Alex began to transform. The insults subsided, and instead, he started to joke around with Mr. Jackson. He stopped pushing every limit and settled into the routine of the class. The rest of the class followed suit, and within a few weeks, the positive learning environment was back. The teacher had been tested and found trustworthy. Alex could settle into the safety of the relationship, and it became a catalyst for a lot of healing and growth for this hurting student.

To think, it all came down to a simple Q-tip.

> You will maintain your happiness as a special education teacher much more easily when you realize that the negative behavior of others is not about you, but rather, there are countless intervening factors involved.

The Q-tip acronym offers a helpful acronym to preserve your health and wholeness as a teacher. We indeed need to Quit Taking Things Personally when we struggle with the actions of others. We live in a world of strong opinions. Social media is rife with angry people fighting over their personal pet perspective. In special education, we have to learn to let go of our tendency to take things personally, even when they seem to be an affront to everything we stand for. **You will maintain your happiness as a special education teacher much more easily when you realize that the negative behavior of others is not about you, but rather, there are countless intervening factors involved.** Table 9.1 offers examples of the Q-tip strategy in special education practice. Teacher Tool 41 provides an activity titled Reflections on the Q-tip Strategy which invites you to consider how this approach may assist you in sustaining your love for your students.

TABLE 9.1 Examples of the Q-Tip Mindset.

Situation Involving Difficulty in Special Education	Unproductive Response From Special Education Teacher (Stress-Producing)	Productive Response Using the Q-tip Mindset (Stress-Busting)
An overtired student is struggling to stay awake during direct instruction.	View this as active disrespect. Rouse the student and admonish the behavior in front of the group.	Investigate why the student is so sleepy through a private conversation. Plan for rest breaks if needed.
A student expresses loud complaints when asked to write a paragraph about who is in the student's family and what they like to do for fun.	View this as intentional disruption of the learning environment. Write a referral and send the student to the office for insubordination, demanding that the principal assign a consequence.	Come alongside the student and quietly ask how you can help. Realize that this student may not have strong writing skills or may not wish to share about his family.
A student has promised you he will stop getting into verbal altercations in the lunchroom. He gets into another argument the next day during lunch.	Become downtrodden and defeated. Assume that your efforts with this student have been in vain, and perhaps you weren't cut out for special education after all. Begin to give up on the student.	Realize that the student doesn't have the skills to meet the social demands of the lunchroom setting. Explore his needs and provide a new plan for lunchtime.
A student becomes frustrated with a math problem and says, 'I hate this school, and I hate you!'	Feel upset and sad that the student hates you and rack your brain for ways to win the student over again, dwelling on this all evening.	Take a look at the math skill which caused the student to become upset and make a plan for a different instructional approach for this area.

Teacher Tool 41: Reflections on the Q-TIP Strategy

In special education, it can be challenging to de-personalize negative student behavior. However, taking things personally can create stress and difficulty. Complete the reflection below to consider how you might practice the Q-TIP Strategy: **'Quit Taking It Personally'** when struggling with an interaction.

What are some student behaviors which 'get under your skin' or cause you to take personal offense? Why do you think these bother you so much?
What are some words of positive self-talk you can utilize 'in the moment' if you find yourself taking a student's negative behavior personally?
When you find yourself 'stuck' on a particular negative interaction with a student, how might you shift your mindset back to a positive outlook?
How might the Q-TIP Strategy help you sustain your own love for the profession of special education and preserve your relationships with students?

Kind, Not Permissive

We have all learned about the importance of relationships with students. One mistake that I have seen many teachers make is to become overly permissive. In the name of relationship-building, they become more of a friend than a teacher. YIKES. No. Just. No. This is not the idea. Being a kind, relational teacher does not mean you have to say yes to everything students want, or start starring in their TikToks if you aren't comfortable with this, or spend your life savings buying them snacks every day.

I have been guilty of this myself. Early in my career, I was more of a 'buddy' or a 'pal' than a teacher. I was teaching at the middle school level, and my caseload and classes were largely composed of young ladies who were identified in the area of emotional/behavior disorders. They were each fabulous in their own way, but when pulled together as a group, they could turn into a pack of fierce lionesses, and I looked like a sickly zebra limping along the savannah. To put it briefly, I was eaten alive. Why? Because I was much more concerned with them liking me than I was with their learning. We all want to be liked. It's natural. We also think that in order to be a relationship-based teacher, we need our students to approve of our decisions. This is incorrect.

Over my years in education, I have learned that setting boundaries and helping students follow them actually helps relationships. They don't want a permissive teacher, even if they think they do. Helping them understand how to function in the school setting is part of our job. We can guide them toward their own sense of right and wrong through our relationships as we bring out the best in them. Being a relational teacher doesn't mean we let go of expectations in our classroom, and it doesn't mean we ignore unacceptable behavior. In fact, when we become pushovers just so students will like us, we completely lose their respect, and it harms the relationship.

Today I have learned that being a relationship-based teacher is all about balance. On one side of the scale is my warmth, kindness, caring, and genuine love for each student. On the other side is my expectation that they do what is right, follow the basic guidelines expected of them at school, and operate as decent human beings in my classroom. I show students that I trust them to have a sense of right and wrong inside of themselves, and I believe in them to choose the high road. We talk about this openly in my classroom, and I recognize that what is right and wrong will be different depending on their environment. The right choice at home may not be right at school. The right choice at school may not be right in the workplace someday. Through caring and kindness, we connect, and then I can guide them toward growth in their ability to manage the accountability present in the school setting. Never, ever do I give in or become overly permissive, but everything is enforced with one message in mind: we are in this together, and I care about your success.

While students may think they want a permissive teacher and the chance to do whatever they want, in truth, they experience a greater sense of security when simple rules are in place. Helping students understand how to function in the school setting is part of the work of special education teachers. Well-established rules can help prevent problem behavior and improve achievement outcomes for students as they learn to function within these parameters (Aelterman et al., 2019). You might liken the rules in the classroom to speed limits which keep people safe on the roads. Many people don't like the fact that there are speed limits, but without them, there would be serious safety concerns and ultimately chaos. Some rules and boundaries are necessary on the roads, and this is also the case at school. Note that I definitely have been guilty of having a lead foot.

> Being a relational teacher doesn't mean that you let go of expectations in your learning environments, and it doesn't mean that you ignore unacceptable behavior.

Being a relational teacher doesn't mean that you let go of expectations in your learning environments, and it doesn't mean that you ignore unacceptable behavior. Rather, you can act as a caring adult and a guide to appropriate behavior at school. Students need both. Table 9.2 offers examples of the difference between a kind yet permissive response and a kind and consistent response to various classroom situations.

Expectations for your students vary across settings, and this can be confusing for them (and for all of us). An important aspect

TABLE 9.2 Kind and Permissive vs. Kind and Consistent.

Situation in Special Education	Kind and Permissive Response	Kind and Consistent Response
A student is throwing tiny bits of paper at you while you are teaching.	Laugh along with the class and act like you enjoy the student's antics. Choose to ignore the behavior although it is creating a distraction.	Invite students to pair up and discuss a question. Discreetly address the student throwing the paper and ask them to please stop.
A student arrives at class ten minutes late every day with no explanation.	Ignore it and pretend the student is on time— don't mark her tardy or question the behavior to avoid issues.	Chat privately with the student about why she is often late. Help her plan to be on time and explain that being on time is a helpful habit for her future.
A student frequently uses profanity during class. It's not aggressive, but it's not appropriate.	Allow the student to use the words he wants to use so that he can be himself. If this includes profanity, that's part of who he is.	Individually discuss this with the student and help him understand the expectations in the school context. Express empathy and understanding but ask him to refrain from using profanity.
A student asks for bathroom passes and leaves class for 20–30 minutes at a time. She returns with fresh makeup on.	Assume that the student must have stomach issues and needs the long bathroom breaks. Ignore the lengthy time she is leaving class, and hope that she still picks up on the learning.	Chat with the student about the missed class time and express that you miss her when she is gone. Help her plan to shorten the breaks and to put on her makeup before school. Use kindness and humor.

of instruction for special education teachers is that of contextual expectations. Students navigate many different worlds, such as school, home, and perhaps the workplace for older students, and each of these environments involves varying expectations for conduct. Students probably experience vastly different expectations from class to class at the secondary level. Helping students to recognize the unwritten rules which exist across settings can support their success overall.

> Students need the opportunity to identify exactly what is expected of them between the settings they navigate and build the skills to manage these shifting requirements.

Students need the opportunity to identify exactly what is expected of them between the settings they navigate and build the skills to manage these shifting requirements. This may involve both direct instruction and modeling, depending on the student and the situation. Teacher Tool 42 offers an activity titled The Unwritten Rules, which you can complete with your students to help develop this understanding and support students in meeting unspoken expectations. As you explore the unwritten rules with students, you help convey the importance of boundaries. This balances relational interaction with structure and accountability in the learning environment. Students must learn that boundaries matter in order to survive and thrive as adults. So stop being their bestie and start being their tour guide to the many expectations in the worlds they experience!

Behaviors Are Messages

Layla Jackson often dreaded professional development days because, to be honest, she got bored quite easily. She had so much to do in her classroom, the last thing she wanted to do was sit and listen to a speaker talk. Gearing up for the day, she filled her purse with snacks and planned to multitask on her laptop all day to make productive use of her time.

Layla arrived just in time to grab a seat in the back row, ready to check out and ignore the day's training. She knew this wasn't a good attitude, but she just didn't have the time to pay attention. Her school year hadn't been going too well, and it was only October. A few of her students were really struggling in their general education classes, and the teachers were starting to complain to her about the need for solutions. As the case manager, the pressure was on to offer some tools to help the students, but Layla's toolbox was feeling a little empty. She knew she should probably listen to the training today to gather some ideas, but instead she just wanted to get things done. The topic for the day was something related to behavior, so perhaps she would pick up something helpful from the speaker, Dr. Jacki Harper.

Teacher Tool 42: The Unwritten Rules

Think about the different expectations you need to follow at school, at home, or in another setting you go to often. Consider the guidelines you follow for what you do and say in these different places. Then, go back and notice the differences. When and how do you change what you do and say in order to follow expectations?

Expectations at School:	
List the rules you follow for what you do and say at school which may not be the 'official' written rules in the handbook.	
Expectations at Home:	
List the rules you follow for what you do and say at home which may be different from the rules at school	
Expectations at _____:	
Choose another setting you go to often. List the rules you follow in this setting for what you do and say.	

Dr. Harper entered the room with a can of Diet Coke in her hand.

'Good morning, everyone, and thanks for coming. I know these professional development days aren't always your favorite, but I'll try to make this as painless as possible.' She then went on to introduce herself and explain her qualifications with warmth and humor.

'Okay,' Layla thought. 'Maybe this lady will be interesting.' She decided to give her a chance and pay attention.

Dr. Harper then wordlessly set her Diet Coke on the table and asked, 'Could I get a volunteer to come up here, please?'

An eager-looking woman in the front row raised her hand with excitement and approached the front platform.

'What would you like me to do?' asked the volunteer.

'Okay, I need you to do me a favor. I need you to shake this can as hard as you can. I mean really get into it. Can you do that for me?'

'Well, sure!' said the volunteer, picking up the can and shaking it with vigor for about 30 seconds, evoking chuckles from the crowd.

When the volunteer set the can down, Dr. Harper picked it up without missing a beat and instantly cracked it open. With a loud fizz, foam and brown liquid exploded out of the can and dripped down her hand and arm onto the floor, even splashing her pale blue blouse.

A few gasps could be heard among the crowd.

'Okay, she's got my attention now,' thought Layla.

Dr. Harper stood, still and smiling, as the stream of soda stopped flowing from the can. The whole thing was quite a unique sight to behold. The room was silent, all eyes focused on what would happen next.

'Now,' said Dr. Harper when she finally spoke. 'As you can see, my soda exploded all over me, and I have quite a mess on my hands. Question. Was I the one to shake the can?'

'No,' murmured some members of the crowd.

'But I'm the one with the mess. Well, I hate to break it to you, but this is often how it goes with our students. Life is happening to them outside of our classroom, and for many of them, life is shaking up their soda can. Sometimes as teachers, we are the ones who come along and crack it open. What does this mean? It means that we need to stay patient with students and help them clean up their messes so they can get on with their day. Today we will be talking about strategies to build

resilience in students and help them manage their personal difficulties so they can best manage the demands of school.'

Layla was hooked. Rather than multitasking, she took copious notes on ways she could help students. She left the training with some strategies she could implement immediately. She absolutely loved the soda can analogy, and it helped her to keep things in perspective when her students had an emotional outburst.

Whenever she was feeling stressed, she cracked an ice-cold Diet Coke and remembered not to let herself get too shaken up!

Dr. Harper's illustration shows us that there are many factors which influence student actions which are outside of our control. How do we help them? We try to figure out what they need, and then we provide it. Simple as that. Students are communicating all day long whether they are speaking or not. Their actions are often their expression of their truths, and much can be learned from careful observation of their interactions and patterns. Rather than reacting to behavior as something to be feared, you will be a much more peaceful teacher if you view it as another form of communication. What is this student trying to tell me? How can I meet the unmet need? You will increase the likelihood of emotional health when you realize that although you cannot 'control' student behavior and stop negative events entirely, you can identify elements of the environment which may incite undesirable behavior and take steps to reduce these triggers.

> Students are communicating all day long whether they are speaking or not. Their actions are often their expression of their truths, and much can be learned from careful observation of their interactions and patterns.

When you view behavior as communication, you realize that rather than consequences or punishment, the student might just need some instruction. Teaching them the skills to change their negative behaviors before they start is SO REWARDING and can change a student's life in perpetuity. Nothing will create frustration faster for both you and your students than trying to punish or assign consequences to change behavior when the unmet need in the student remains. In addition to a missing skill, perhaps there is a missing resource the student needs in a physical, emotional, or academic sense. When special educators listen to the unspoken messages in student behavior, they can offer what students really need and realize the lasting rewards which come from transformative special education (Jeong and Copeland, 2019).

There are countless unseen triggers which impact student engagement in their school day, and these are often out of the educator's control. At times, students will not be at their best due to temporary conditions in their lives. At other times, students will come to the classroom with a longer history of trauma which impacts their overall functioning, including their engagement in their education. Temporary states of discomfort in physical, mental, or emotional health will be common among students.

The HALTS acronym may be helpful to special education teachers trying to identify why a student is out of sorts or experiencing an undesirable state of being, standing for Hungry, Angry, Lonely, Tired, and Stressed (Turner, 2018). Students in any of these states may be more likely to enact undesirable behaviors because they have immediate unmet needs. Teacher Tool 43 offers an activity titled HALTS Interventions, which special education teachers can complete to support students through these difficulties. It is of note that teachers may also use the HALTS acronym to reflect on their own feelings and meet their own needs in order to maintain health, wholeness, and stability.

For many students, difficulties with emotional, mental, and physical health will extend beyond temporary experiences. Traumatic experiences may have impacted their lens on life and their interaction with the world in general. Trauma is defined as a very difficult or unpleasant experience that causes someone to have mental or emotional problems usually for a long time (Merriam-Webster, 2021). Students in special education have often endured traumatic events in their personal histories, and this impacts their experience of learning and can create difficulties in the school environment (Spencer, 2019).

When you work with students who have a history of significant trauma, your Q-Tip and soda can mentality can help prevent the pain of personalization and burnout. The trauma of the past will inevitably create challenges for the student, and they particularly rely on consistent, stalwart educators dedicated to supporting them in their learning journey. No pressure! To

Teacher Tool 43: H.A.L.T.S. Interventions

Students may come to your instruction sessions or classes **hungry, angry, lonely, tired, or sick**. They cannot learn best in these difficult conditions. Complete this form to plan for how you may identify and meet these needs to prevent undesirable behaviors or outcomes for students in these situations.

Hungry: What are some resources you can utilize for hungry students?
Angry: How might you help a student who arrives at school or class angry?
Lonely: How might you help a student who expresses that they are feeling lonely?
Tired: How might you help a student who arrives at school or class tired?
Stressed: What will be your course of action for students who are feeling stressed?

succeed with students who have endured trauma, you must first tend to your personal needs (see Chapter 3). You can also bring in strategies to help students take good loving care of their own hearts. This may include instruction on self-regulation strategies, mindfulness practices, and grounding techniques (again, reference Chapter 3).

> It's up to us as teachers to convey that struggling students are safe, accepted, and can be comfortable in our learning spaces.

Students may be living, breathing, and having their full life experience in a state of stress. We've all heard of the fight-flight-freeze response, which may be activated when the brain senses danger. Well, some of our students are living in this space. It's tough to learn when you are fighting, fleeing, or frozen. It's up to us as teachers to convey that struggling students are safe, accepted, and can be comfortable in our learning spaces. Not easy to do, but once we create a happy haven for a student, we can see tremendous growth and success! Teacher Tool 44 offers a safety plan you can complete with a student to help create a sense of safety for them at school. This exercise has been invaluable to me over the years and has never been more important in my practice.

Another powerful practice you can use for all students to reduce difficulty is to help them identify their day-to-day triggers in the school setting. Once aware of what bothers them, students can better recognize their rising emotional responses and activate strategies to calm down. Both teachers and students can benefit from awareness of what sets them off so that they can avoid these situations or take self-protective measures to prepare when triggers are unavoidable. In my small groups and classes, we used to take time early in the school year to share about what got on our nerves so that we could come together and agree that we would try not to do these things.

Perhaps this sounds like a bad idea. Didn't students try to push each other's buttons? Thankfully no, because everyone was a part of the conversation. If I know your buttons, you know mine, so let's call a truce. This helped learning happen, and it helped us all avoid stress! Teacher Tool 45 offers a form you can use with your students titled What Bothers Me, which invites

Teacher Tool 44: Safety Plan

This is an individual plan teachers and students can create together to help identify pathways to calmness. Answer the questions below together and use the plan to help make school a safe, positive experience!

When do you feel most upset during the day?

What usually makes you upset during the day?

What are some words or actions the student will use when feeling upset?

What are some words or actions the teacher will use to help the student calm down?

What are some strategies the student can use to calm down?

How will the teacher help the student with these strategies?

Teacher Tool 45: What Bothers Me?

Complete this form to identify some of the things that make you upset.
Include your typical responses, whether positive or negative. Think about
the words and actions of others that make you upset, as well as common
situations which cause you to struggle. This will help your teacher create a
better school experience for you.

Things that bother me at school	My typical responses

them to share their peeves so they don't have to feel so peevish
in your learning spaces. Try to have fun with this, because it can
actually bring out lots of laughs!

Preserving Relationships

Before we leave this chapter, I have a few more gems to share
which have helped me keep loving special education, even

when I was working with students who struggled with challenging behaviors. I learned early on that preserving my relationship with each student would be a lifeline for both of us. This meant that at all costs, I would figure out a way to get back into harmony after a difficult behavioral situation. Three tools have helped me achieve this, and I still use them to this day. Just a note, they work with adults too after a challenging interaction.

First, restorative rather than punitive responses. Words like 'obey,' 'respect,' and 'consequence' have become almost meaningless to students. Instead, I always offer the student lots of time to cool down before inviting them into a conversation focused on restoration. The question is, 'How can we make things right again?' Then I zip my lips and listen. Whenever things are tense in any way, I remind myself to use lower volume, speak more slowly, and say less. Cool as a cucumber, I calmly engage the student in a peaceful chat about restoring things to the way they were before the incident.

Second, I help the student repair things with the group. When a negative behavior happens, it can really upset the applecart. Peers may feel nervous around the student or may be irritated about the situation. This is natural. I help the student reestablish acceptance in the group by ushering him or her back in and emphasizing their good traits and qualities. Trying not to make it too obvious, I express the key message to the student: 'I see you . . . I like you . . . and I'm glad you're here,' even after a challenging behavioral incident. The group most often follows suit with my example.

Finally, I exercise amnesia. What was that? I forgot. Oh yes. Amnesia. I erase the incident from my mind to the greatest extent possible. This can be challenging and even somewhat unnatural, but it is so important to maintaining my connection with the student. I do not bring up the situation ever again, and I fully move on. If the student mentions it, I change the subject quickly and focus on the good things happening in the here and now. This has been a powerful and effective practice in preserving relationships over the years. Table 9.3 provides further details and examples on relationship life-preservers.

TABLE 9.3 Relationship Life-Preservers With Examples.

Teacher Strategies	Examples in Special Education
Restorative Practices: After a challenging situation, support the student in making things right in order to move on in a positive way. The student may brainstorm ideas with the special education teacher's guidance. Note that forced apologies have no place in education.	After destroying a classroom bulletin board in anger, a student explains that she was feeling upset about an argument with her sister that morning. She learns a phrase she can say to explain that she is upset and helps to create a new bulletin board along with other students who volunteer to help.
Relationship Repair: After a negative incident, the special education teacher expresses that the student is a valued member of the class and reminds them that they bring many positive aspects to the group. Engage in casual conversation about other topics of interest to restore rapport. This stage is incredibly powerful in that it conveys unconditional acceptance.	When a student returns to school the day after a negative incident, the special education teacher communicates the message 'I see you, I like you, I'm glad you're here,' through both words and actions. The special education teacher engages the group in a preferred activity (such as a game) which demands social interaction and evokes fun and laughter.
Amnesia: Also called motivated forgetting, individuals choose to leave the past in the past and focus on the present moment or the possibilities for the future. Let go of the negativity and, after restorative practices, move on as if it never happened. Students benefit greatly when they are offered the grace of a clean slate.	After a negative incident, a special education teacher engages the student in restorative practices and relationship repair. Once resolved, the special educator intentionally chooses to forget about the event and focus on offering the student a fresh start. The teacher also encourages the student to leave the negative event in the past and focus on the here and now, as well as a positive future.

Conclusion

Approach classroom management with the knowledge that if you are there to love kids and support them, they will sense this and engage in a positive way. Have FUN with your students! Boredom is not your friend in any way, shape, or form. Help engage your students by identifying the leaders among your group and hooking them from the get-go. Remember that you can be a kind, caring, genuine, relational teacher without being permissive. In fact, most students want the safety of accountability, not a doormat. It shows that you care when you help them meet high expectations. Even when difficulties occur and emotions run high, strive to de-escalate situations as much as you can. Your response in-the-moment can make or break the trajectory of an incident. Keep cool, and your students will follow.

Remember to Q-Tip, or Quit Taking It Personally, as much as you can, realizing that student behavior is most often not about you. Other factors shook up the soda can, and you were the lucky sap who opened it to take a sip. Remember that every day is a fresh start with every student and that you all have the same goals in the long run: creating happy, healthy adults! Managing a classroom can be unpredictable and challenging, but your students will benefit from your consistent, supportive presence. Create a safe space, build their self-regulation skills, and if things go awry, a bit of amnesia never hurt anyone. Lead with your heart and hold fast to your commitment to love students, even through the most trying interactions. You will discover that this helps students change for the better!

Navigating Classroom Management

- ◆ Remember that boredom begets behavior, so try to keep students engaged.
- ◆ Don't take it personally when students struggle—it's usually not really about you.
- ◆ Being kind and relational doesn't mean you don't enforce boundaries.
- ◆ Be proactive by watching out for HALTS: Hungry, Angry, Lonely, Tired, and Sick.
- ◆ Identify what bothers your students and then take steps to prevent their triggers.
- ◆ Take steps to preserve relationships to preserve your sanity!

Reflection Questions

Use the following questions to reflect on what you have learned in the chapter. You may choose to journal about them or discuss them with a partner or small group to gain further insights.

1. Which elements of engagement do you plan to utilize? How might this help your students?
2. What are your thoughts on the Q-tip strategy? How do negative classroom incidents typically impact you? How do you care for yourself after difficulty?
3. How might you work with students to create guidelines and expectations for classroom conduct? How might you help students understand the unwritten rules in this context?
4. What are your thoughts on the premise that behavior is communication? How do you connect with the soda can analogy?
5. How does the soda can analogy help you understand student behavior? How might the acronym HALTS help you support students with difficulty? How might you implement trauma-informed practices for students who have a more challenging history?
6. What are your preferred strategies for preserving relationships? How might the tools in this chapter support your sustained connections with students?

References

Aelterman, N., Vansteenkiste, M., & Haerens, L. (2019). Correlates of students' internalization and defiance of classroom rules: A self-determination theory perspective. *British Journal of Educational Psychology*, vol. 89, no. 1, Wiley-Blackwell, pp. 22–40, https://doi.org/10.1111/bjep.12213.

Jeong, Y., & Copeland, S. R. (2019). Comparing functional behavior assessment-based interventions and non-functional behavior assessment-based interventions: A systematic review of outcomes and methodological quality of studies. *Journal of Behavioral Education*, vol. 29, no. 1, pp. 1–41, https://doi.org/10.1007/s10864-019-09355-4.

Merriam-Webster. (2021). Trauma. In *Merriam-Webster.com*. Retrieved October 28, 2021, from https://www.merriam-webster.com/dictionary/trauma.

Spencer, S. (2019). What about us? Vicarious trauma in our 'systems' [Dissertation, Lynn University]. Student Theses, Dissertations, Portfolios and Projects. https://spiral.lynn.edu/etds/353.

Turner, C. (2018). How are you feeling? Take a minute to HALT for your health. *Goodtherapy.org*. www.goodtherapy.org/blog/how-are-you-feeling-take-minute-halt-for-your-health-0515184.

10

Gratitude, Acceptance, and Purpose

Ms. Salish would be instructing in the extended school year summer school program for students with cognitive disabilities in her district. In the summer school environment, each student would be arriving with different goals, and it was up to her to help them make progress. It could be a challenge to create lessons and materials to meet all their needs. It could also be difficult to build relationships with them and among them in such a short time. Not to mention the fact that she would need to take data on all their goals, communicate with parents, figure out accommodations and modifications . . . Okay. Whew. What had she gotten herself into? At least she would have the support of two seasoned paraprofessionals.

The first day of summer school arrived, and thankfully the bus route successfully picked up all her students, and they filed into the classroom. Much to her surprise, they wore huge smiles. They looked excited to be at school even though it was summertime. She knew the most important factor in their learning this summer would be the creation of positive relationships, so she planned to start each day with a brief morning meeting. Students could build their communication skills by asking and answering questions as they got to know each other. It was worth the time investment, and she hoped students would enjoy it.

The topic for the first morning meeting was a simple question: 'What do you like about summer?' Ms. Salish invited students to sit in a circle around a table. She asked the student next to her, James,

DOI: 10.4324/9781003322528-11

to say his name and answer the question, 'What do you like about summer?' Much to her delight, he had a definitive answer. Hot dogs. His favorite thing about summer was hot dogs. Many other students spoke up in agreement. Kalia, a shy student who rarely spoke, explained that she preferred a cheeseburger. They were off to the races building new connections over the topic of summer grilling. Perfect! James then asked the student next to him, 'What's your name, and what do you like about summer?' So the conversation continued, loaded with laughs, smiles, and connections!

Each day, students seemed to look forward to the meeting before transitioning into 'work time.' The smiles kept coming, and many expressed that the morning meeting was their favorite part of the day. What seemed like a piece of pedagogical 'fluff' was proving to be invaluable. The routine helped students wake up their brains and settle in. Their communication skills were growing as well. For example, a student who often spoke very softly grew in confidence and spoke up without prompting. A student who struggled with expressive language was putting his thoughts into words more quickly through the daily conversations. More and more, everyone was coming out of their shells, and Ms. Salish loved it! She found the students to be funny, kind, and honestly delightful.

Before she knew it, the last day of summer programming arrived. Ms. Salish found it bittersweet. She was ready for a little rest to recharge for the school year. Waking up without an alarm clock would be lovely. However, she would miss the little summer school family which had developed. She had achieved the warm, happy vibe she hoped for, just as she did each and every school year in the fall. It helped that the students were absolutely fantastic individuals.

The morning meeting would look a little different on the last day. Instead of asking a question, Ms. Salish was planning to hold a 'compliment circle,' in which each student takes a turn receiving compliments from the rest of the group. This activity would accomplish many hidden social objectives for the students. Those giving the compliments would need to come up with kind things to say, which is something anyone can work on. Those receiving the compliments get to work on receiving kindness, which can sometimes present difficulty.

'Okay, let's start our meeting today,' Ms. Salish said, pulling the group together. They took their places around the circle. The first student, Alex, scooted his chair up to the table. 'Today's meeting is going to be a little bit different. Instead of answering a question, we are going to be giving some compliments. Does anyone know what a compliment is?'

'It's when you say something nice about someone,' said Kalia.

'Exactly right. So we're going to start with Alex. Anyone can chime in. So here is my question: What do we like about Alex?'

It was as if the room had exploded. Everyone started talking at once and among the voices, phrases like 'He's a great helper,' and 'He's funny,' and 'He's an awesome friend' could be heard. Ms. Salish almost had to laugh. She hadn't expected the students to be so eager to pipe up and to have so much to say! This love-fest continued as they made their way around the circle discussing each student. Students offered compliments, which were specific and accurate, revealing the genuine relationships which had been built over the summer. Ms. Salish thought to herself, 'Well, I guess this couldn't have gone any better!' As the meeting wrapped up with the last student and the group prepared to transition to work time, our special education teacher asked a reflective question.

'Wow, what was it like to give and receive all those compliments?'

The room was quiet for a moment, and then Kalia spoke up.

'I have to say, my heart melted like cheese,' she said with a soft giggle.

And Ms. Salish's heart melted too, like cheese.

> Being a special education teacher offers each of us the chance to become the very best, most-fulfilled human beings we can possibly be.

Ms. Salish rose to the challenge of running a summer school program and experienced the deeply moving rewards which come from building community and spreading genuine love among students. Learners grew in their abilities, and Ms. Salish grew in her love for the profession. Teaching special education is a job like no other. We have the opportunity to build relationships with students and families which can truly transform lives. Many of our students and parents come to us feeling chewed up and spit out by the experience of education. We have the chance to give hope and bring healing, and it's just so absolutely amazing. Sure, being a special education teacher is demanding, overwhelming, and exhausting at times. But the truth of the matter is, being a special education teacher offers each of us the chance to become the very best, most-fulfilled human beings we can possibly be.

Always remember that your students are your best teachers! You will learn more from them than any professional development day or book (haha), if you only pay attention. Implement, observe, and reflect in an ongoing cycle, and you will grow as a teacher every day. The minute we think we have this job all figured out is the minute we start to stagnate. Keep your heart for teaching alive as you are energized by students! Thus, we arrive at the heart of this whole book, and here it is: infuse your practice with gratitude, accept the challenge before you, stick to your purpose, and hold fast to your commitment to your students.

> Infuse your practice with gratitude, accept the challenge before you, stick to your purpose, and hold fast to your commitment to your students.

How do we put this into practice in the special education world? Well, this will look different for everyone. For me, it begins with patience. Be patient with yourself, with your students, and with the situations that challenge you. Sometimes there isn't an instant fix, and I need to allow time and space for things to work themselves out. Another key element for me is gentleness and a soft heart across the board. It's easy to become critical of ourselves, our colleagues, and our students, but it serves no one.

Every day as I'm driving to work, I take a breath and remind myself that an open, kind heart is the best thing I can bring to my students each day. If you are rolling your eyes at the cheesiness of this, I understand, but I also invite you to see what happens if you decide that your main job is to show up at school and love kids all day. I promise you, your job will become a blast! Your students will bask in the glow of your consistent kindness, and you will bring out the best in them. Just typing these sentences makes me excited to be a special education teacher for years and years and years to come. What could be better?

Every single day I have spent in the classroom, something amazing and wonderful has happened as long as I look for it with a heart of gratitude. Sometimes it's something obvious. Everyone aces a test or masters a skill. My students are getting along and exchanging spontaneous compliments. Nothing short of miraculous. Sometimes the wins are less obvious. The student who is struggling keeps showing up. The most reluctant learner finally buys in. The coffee in my cup tastes delicious. My point? There is something good in every day if you look at it. We have to view our jobs through the lens of the positive and harvest the gold hidden in our day-to-day activity with students. I promise you it's there. I also can almost guarantee that the longer you are working in special education, the harder it can be to find those positive gems hidden within each day. There will be times when you are bogged down by the demands of the job. You will feel that you are mopping the deck on the *Titanic* or shoveling diamonds into a black hole. Don't believe these jaded thoughts. The truth is, as long as you keep showing up and doing your best, you are making an impact. Your students are depending on your ability to filter out all the negative garbage that can bog you down in education and hold tightly to the belief that all students can succeed in the presence of a truly consistent and caring educator.

> Your students are depending on your ability to filter out all the negative garbage that can bog you down in education and hold tightly to the belief that all students can succeed in the presence of a truly consistent and caring educator.

This chapter will explore questions which may bring special education teachers closer to their own hearts, helping them repeatedly ignite their own passion for teaching even when the flame seems to dim. Such questions include the following:

- ◆ How do gratitude practices shape perception and neurological responses to patterns and situations?
- ◆ What is the role of shared gratitude in creating a healthy classroom community? How might both teachers and students engage in regular gratitude practices?
- ◆ How might special education teachers change their trajectory when they find themselves experiencing a downward spiral?
- ◆ What are some ways unconditional acceptance may be applied to situations in order to improve perceptions and outcomes?
- ◆ What does it mean to teach from a place of established identity and confidence? How might this support special education teachers?

♦ How might a sense of purpose help special education teachers overcome challenges and sustain hope?

Just as an athlete engages in regular training to perform well in their sport, you can embrace the practices in this chapter to prepare yourself to manage the emotional and personal challenges presented by this difficult, albeit noble, work. Refining thinking patterns with a focus on gratitude, acceptance, and purpose may equip you to love your students well and avoid burnout.

The Impact of Gratitude

> We can make sure that they receive the message that their differences will not prevent them from becoming fully accepted, cherished, included members of society.

No child wakes up one day and decides 'I'd like to have a disability.' Students in special education are some of the most resilient, strong, tenacious individuals in the entire human race. They are coping with challenges they didn't choose on a daily basis. This means surmounting obstacles few of us can imagine. Unfortunately, the world can be a cold and uncaring place for those who are identified as 'different,' and our students continuously experience stigma and marginalization. What a gift we can give them when we view them as fully capable, valuable human beings. We can make sure that they receive the message that their differences will not prevent them from becoming fully accepted, cherished, included members of society.

I decided very early in my career that I would not be complicit in a system which tells students they are incapable of anything. Doggedly believing in students is a part of my daily life as a special education teacher, and I have found that students respond by succeeding. They want to prove me right when I believe in them with my whole heart, and they do. Over and over and over, I have seen students break down walls to find success beyond expectations because we both believed it could happen. There is absolutely nothing better than helping a student surprise everyone with their successes. Honestly, I live for

it. And you can too, special education teacher. In fact, I hope
you do!

> Gratitude erases frustration
> and helps us send the powerful
> message: I am so glad to be
> your teacher.

This brings us to a revolutionary idea: we can be grateful for
every facet of our student's existence. We can be grateful for every
strength and grateful for every
challenge. Gratitude erases frustration and helps us send the powerful message: I am so glad to
be your teacher. When looking at life through the lens of gratitude, individuals place their focus on what is going well rather
than what is creating difficulty. Psychologically, it's been proven
that people who commit to reframing their experiences from a
perspective of gratitude experience more positive emotions,
healthier relationships, and lower levels of stress (Watkins et al.,
2014; Wood et al., 2009). You will be happier, healthier, and more
content if you learn to start your day in gratitude and stay there
as much as you can.

You may be thinking, 'Now wait a minute, Rachel. You want
me to be thankful for things that stress me out and wear me
down?' Not exactly. I am suggesting that you don't spend your
time fixating on these things. Sure, negative thoughts will float
by like clouds in the sky (see Chapter 3), but you can shift your
eyes to the things that are GOOD because I promise you, there
is ALWAYS something good going on. We can choose to see it.
Gratitude is powerful, and numerous practices have been identified by research to bolster a regular mindset of gratitude, including
practices such as creating gratitude lists and expressing thanks to
others (Ruini, 2017; Joseph and Wood, 2010; Toepfer et al., 2012).
Figure 10.1 provides examples of gratitude practices special education teachers and students may utilize to cultivate a more positive mindset.

Teacher Tool 46 provides a structured activity titled Weekly
Gratitude Journal for Special Education Teachers, which educators
can use to engage in this life-giving activity. A regular gratitude
practice can also have significant positive outcomes for students.
Special education teachers who encourage students to exercise
their gratitude muscle may be pleasantly surprised with what

Teacher Tool 46: Weekly Gratitude Journal

For Special Education Teachers

Pause each day to list three things you appreciate. Strive to think of new things each day to exercise your 'gratitude muscle.' Focus on the immaterial as much as possible.

MONDAY		

TUESDAY		

WEDNESDAY		

THURSDAY		

FRIDAY		

Teacher Tool 47:

students share and may learn more about their students when they invite gratitude sharing into the classroom (Griffith, 2014). Teacher Tool 47 offers an activity titled What Is GOOD Today? which students may complete to cultivate thankfulness and recognize the good!

The U-Turn

There are two things I have found true in my experience as a special education teacher: First, no matter how well things are going, things will never be completely smooth, and there will always be bumps in the road. Second, you can learn and practice the ability to turn things around even on difficult days. I have learned that in any moment, I can stop, reflect, and shift from stuck in the muck to positive and optimistic. Optimism, or the ability to look on the bright side and expect good things, is a powerful mindset which can help us greatly in our practice. Even better? Cultivating a lifestyle of optimism in which this becomes our natural state of being. This can take training and practice, but it is so worth it. Optimists expect the good to occur and tend to experience less stress than their more pessimistic counterparts, and extensive research supports the importance of optimism for individuals with disabilities and special education teachers (Wehmeyer, 2013). Taking time to develop the habits of optimism can set the stage for successfully snapping out of it when the day is not unfolding the way we want it to.

Our brains are designed to keep us safe. It's simple biology. This means that our minds are constantly scanning the environment for threats and problems. This made perfect sense to our ancestors. A simple walk to gather some berries could easily turn fatal if one wasn't scanning the environment for lions, tigers, and bears. Some believe that humans are still wired this way to their very core, even though the direct threat of predatory animals usually doesn't have relevance. Unless perhaps you work at the circus or at the zoo. Understanding that the brain may be hardwired to see the negative does not mean we all have a life sentence to live in pessimism and see the glass as half empty or filled with poison.

> I love my students, I love my work, my basic needs are met, and I am free to choose my mindset. My mental mission is to return to these truths over and over throughout the day.

The easiest way to resist the negativity bias is to be aware that it exists. Once recognized, we can pause and work on making the U-turn, bringing the good things into our awareness and letting the yuck fade away. I do this all the time, sometimes 15 times before breakfast. Not exaggerating! I have made a commitment to myself that I will not ruminate on what is wrong when so much is right in my life. I love my students, I love my work, my basic needs are met, and I am free to choose my mindset. My mental mission is to return to these truths over and over throughout the day. Negative 'stuckness' need not apply. The position of my focus has been filled by the good stuff. Is this easy? Nope! Worth it? Yep! And happily, shifting to the good becomes a habit over time.

When a shift in thinking is in order, as in Rafael's situation, you can follow a simple set of steps as you start out on your optimism journey. The first step may be a mindful pause to return to the present moment and find grounding. What is happening around you in the here and now? Next, think about reality with the purpose of seeing the good. Some call this 'harvesting the gold' from the present moment. Beautiful. Finally, move forward based on the good stuff you discover. Take some sort of action which helps you snap out of the doldrums. Here are a few of my favorite actions which help me make the U-turn when I am having a difficult day:

◆ Chat with a happy student. Take a few minutes to chat with a go-to student who makes you smile. This doesn't mean playing favorites, but we all have that one (or two or three) student(s) who put a smile on our face just from a simple chat. I seek out that student and simply ask how their day is going. We both leave the conversation smiling!

◆ Offer yourself a simple mantra. Grab a sticky note and write down a positive mantra to pump yourself up (see Chapter 3 for details on the power of a simple phrase). One of my favorites for a rough day is 'This isn't as bad as you think.' I also like, 'Look for the good and you will find it.' Basically, I am persuading myself to believe in what I already know.

◆ Appreciate something or someone. Take a spare minute to send a quick thank-you email to someone who has helped you out. Expressing gratitude helps activate the thankful and positive part of your brain. I like to send a quick note of appreciation to the custodian who deals with my messy learning space, or a colleague who has really made a difference. Teaching at the high school level, I can also send a quick thank-you to a student for some kind of positive action. Shooting off an email of gratitude takes all of two minutes, and it brings a smile to both the receiver and the sender—you!

Practicing Acceptance

Difficult situations, emotions, and frustrations are an inevitable part of life. The worst problems of all are those that have no clear solutions. In the world of special education, there are plenty of factors we will not like and we will not be able to change. It's just a fact of the matter. Special education will always involve paperwork. It will always involve challenges with students or families from time to time. There will always be moments in which we feel overwhelmed. How do we handle the unsolvable issues and keep our hearts happy in our work? The answer for me has been acceptance.

> Grant me the serenity to accept the things I cannot change, the courage to change the things I can, and the wisdom to know the difference (**Shapiro, 2014**).

In the early 1930s, ethicist Reinhold Niebuhr composed a creed which has been widely adopted by addition intervention programs, psychologists, philosophers, and counselors which begins, *Grant me the serenity to accept the things I cannot change, the courage to change the things I can, and the wisdom to know the difference* (**Shapiro, 2014**). Whether or not you believe in any sort of higher power, these words may have a powerful impact in that they introduce the concept of acceptance. When I read these words, I realize that if I want peace in my life, I have to learn to accept the things that I just can't change and stop struggling against the things I don't like. This has helped me tremendously in my special education practice. Rather than complaining about the perennial problems which will always exist, I accept them as part of the package, and I don't give them a disproportionate amount of my energy.

Paperwork is a perfect example. In the past, I would stress myself out over each student's file, approaching this part of the work with great disdain. The more I thought about how much I didn't like the minutiae involved in keeping up the paperwork, the less I actually buckled down to complete it. In the time I spent complaining about the paperwork, I could have gotten half of it done. When I learned to practice acceptance, I realized that the paperwork would always be there, and it wasn't worth my frustration. I accepted that in order to complete the parts of the job which I love, teaching my phenomenal students with joy and fun, I would need to accept the parts which weren't my favorite—the paperwork. The funny thing is, once I accepted this, the paperwork didn't seem like such a big deal, and I was able to execute it with renewed motivation. I reframed it as a positive service to protect the rights of students and inform their families, and it no longer loomed large as a daunting negative aspect of my work. Pretty awesome, really!

The quest to resist or fight when facing unchangeable challenges can result in heartache, tension, and angst (Hughes et al., 2019). When situations cannot be changed, spend some time focusing on your inner landscape with the realization that although you cannot control what is happening around you, you can take steps to manage what is happening within. Let go of the battle and surrender your desire for control, focusing instead on cultivating acceptance. The ability to differentiate between what can be changed in a situation and what must be accepted can be difficult. The serenity creed includes a request for discernment, or the 'wisdom to know the difference' (Shapiro, 2014). When you find yourself frustrated or facing burnout, take some time to think about the small changes you could make to improve the situation. This may help you identify the areas in which acceptance is in order because there are no current opportunities to bring about changes.

So what happens when a situation is changeable? After closely examining challenging situations and reflecting on the elements which cannot be changed, special educators may shift their focus to the second section of the serenity creed: 'The courage to change the things I can' (Shapiro, 2014). In some situations, this is indeed an act of courage. Perhaps you realize it is time to take on a new role in their building

> Let go of the battle and surrender your desire for control, focusing instead on cultivating acceptance.

> Is this a real problem or is this a problem I have made up in my head?

or district. Perhaps it is time to confront a personal issue which is encroaching on your ability to focus on your work with students. Maybe it's time for a critical self-advocacy conversation which could result in positive changes (see Chapter 5 for tips on wise advocacy). At times, the changes have little to do with external actions, and they relate to transforming patterns of thought and action which are no longer helpful. I have grown so much when I have stopped to ask the question, 'Is this a real problem or is this a problem I have made up in my head?' I learned to stop creating difficulty for myself where there really was none. 'The courage to change the things I can' meant changing my mindset and my focus. Teacher Tool 48 provides an activity, titled Change vs. Cannot Change, you can use to reflect on what you can and cannot influence to help you practice acceptance.

Teaching With Purpose

We all arrive in special education through our own journey. Some of us set out to become special educators from day one of college. For many, the journey is less of a straight line and more of a labyrinth. This was certainly true for me. When I became a teacher, I had no idea about the world of special education. I was going to be a middle school English teacher. In order to pay the bills and take care of practicum hours, I landed a job as a paraprofessional (also known as an educational assistant) in a program for students with emotional/behavioral disorders. And I was hooked. Starting in August, I knew by the end of October that I would be a special education teacher, and it was right where I belonged. Rather than teaching a large group of students how to write an essay, I got to teach a small group of individuals how to live life. I could cultivate true relationships with every student and family, and I could help them find a path to success despite the challenges presented by their child's disability.

Students with special needs are some of the most creative, kind, brilliant, enjoyable people in my life. We laugh together every single day, and I have learned much more from them than they have learned from me. I cannot tell you how many times

Teacher Tool 48: What Can I Change? What Must I Accept?

Use this form to reflect on the elements of your practice which are within your scope of influence and those you are unable to change.

What can I change and what must I accept?	
Things I can change:	Things I must accept:

Reflection and Application:
What are the most important items on the list of things you can change?
What are some action steps you can take to address these areas?

over the years I have turned to a coworker and said, 'We seriously have the best job.' We do. It's the truth. And you get to enjoy the ride as well, my dear special education teacher. For so many of our students, showing up to school each day is an act of tenacity and resilience. School has been a place of great challenge, and yet, there they sit in their seats each day. This alone inspires me to be the most dedicated and engaged educator I can possibly be.

No matter how you landed in special education, I believe you are here for a reason. There is a student you are meant to reach. There is a life you are meant to impact. With my whole heart, I believe that teaching special education is more than a job; it is a calling and a purpose. No student winds up on my class list or caseload by accident. Each is meant to cross my path so that I can offer my best shot at helping them find a better life.

> No matter how you landed in special education, I believe you are here for a reason. There is a student you were meant to reach. There is a life you were meant to impact.

This is truly what keeps me going and keeps me loving my work every day. Success isn't instant for every student, and there are certainly challenges, but I do believe that most students leave my classroom better off than when they arrived. If our time together improves their experience of life in even small ways, this is something to celebrate. I am so grateful to be a special education teacher every day, and I hope you stay grateful too!

You will thrive in your work when you wake up in the morning with a renewed commitment to make a lasting difference in the lives of your students. No matter how challenging you might find a student's needs, you have a unique opportunity to breathe life into your students and offer a refreshing dose of positive energy. Relentless commitment to unconditional acceptance may offer a foundation for purposeful, life-giving practice. You are doing work that matters every day. You are poised to have a lasting legacy which has a deep impact on another life. I can imagine nothing better!

As we finish up our journey together in these pages, I invite you to spend time reflecting on your purpose. Why are you here in special education? What drives you and inspires you? Teacher Tool 49 involves an activity titled Teaching With Purpose, which invites you to consider your mission as a special educator. Teacher Tool 50 offers another activity you can complete, titled My Legacy, which allows you to envision the many beautiful things you hope

Teacher Tool 49: Teaching with Purpose

Use this reflection to explore your sense of purpose and compose your personal mission statement. Whenever you feel challenged, return to this purpose and mission to help you sustain yourself in special education.

Why did you become a special education teacher?

What do you love most about your special education practice?

What do your students need most from you?

What is your personal mission statement?
Use this sentence frame if necessary:

In order to _____,

I will

_____,

because I value _____.

Teacher Tool 50: My Legacy

Reflect on who you are and your sense of purpose in your special education classroom. Then, use this form to journal about what you want to be known for. Defining what you can offer the world can help you serve students from a place of purpose.

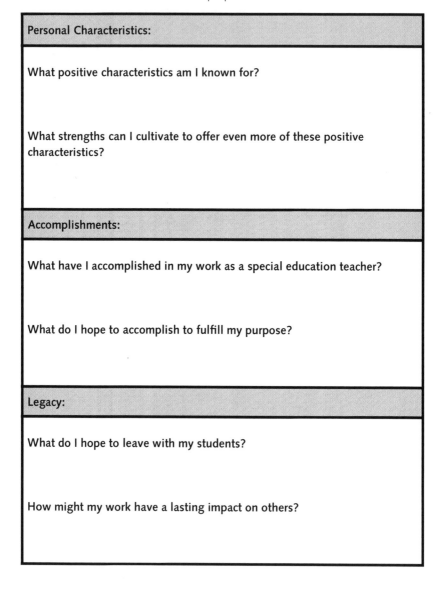

Personal Characteristics:

What positive characteristics am I known for?

What strengths can I cultivate to offer even more of these positive characteristics?

Accomplishments:

What have I accomplished in my work as a special education teacher?

What do I hope to accomplish to fulfill my purpose?

Legacy:

What do I hope to leave with my students?

How might my work have a lasting impact on others?

> You will thrive in your work when you wake up in the morning with a renewed commitment to make a lasting difference in the lives of your students.

to leave with your students. I implore you to return to your purpose, mission, and desired legacy when you feel the burnout creeping up on you. Stay inspired, stay motivated, and most importantly, stay in love with this meaningful work!

Conclusion

You will fall in love with this work when you live in a space of gratitude, acceptance, and purpose. There is always something good happening in your world, and you can harvest the gold at any moment in your special education practice. Learn to accept the aspects of your job which you cannot change, and take heart that none of the problems are as daunting as they may seem. Sometimes, we discover that the lion has no teeth. The things which frighten or stress us out are actually only as problematic as we allow them to be. When you discover something you can change to improve your situation or that of your students, take action with love and empathy.

Most importantly, fully embrace your role in special education as more than a job. Invest yourself in the profession, and let it become part of the fabric of who you are. Wear your role as a special education teacher as a badge of honor and focus on what you love about the special education life and your students!

Recognize that participating in this great profession can be one of the most incredible blessings of your life if you find the beauty in every day! Don't be afraid to actually, truly love your students with a teacherly style of love that is unique to our profession. And here's the thing—that teacherly love is for ALL your students, no matter what, nonnegotiable, every day. You will be energized in your profession when you find a way to delight in every single student. Make it your mission to find the individual brilliance hidden within each kid, because I promise you it's there. Teachers who love students, practice gratitude, and approach their work with a deeper purpose will leave a powerful positive legacy with students and families

Reflection Questions

Use the following questions to reflect on what you have learned in the chapter. You may choose to journal about them or discuss them with a partner or small group to gain further insights.

1. How might the suggestions for gratitude practices support you and your students? Which suggestions are your favorite?
2. How might cultivating optimism help you make a U-turn when you are having a difficult day?
3. What are three go-to actions you can take when you feel stuck in negative thinking?
4. What are some elements of your practice which you must accept? What are some changes you might make?
5. Why did you become a special education teacher, and where do you find a sense of meaning and purpose in your work today?
6. What is the legacy you hope to leave with your students? How might this help to inspire your work when times are tough?

Simple Snapshot

◆ Gratitude is powerful, and there is always something GOOD going on!
◆ At any moment in the day, you can pause and refocus on the positive.
◆ Identify what you cannot change in situations and practice acceptance.
◆ Identify what you can change in situations and take action steps.

- ◆ Find purpose in your practice and you will find yourself inspired!
- ◆ Reflect on the legacy you hope to leave and use this to sustain your heart.
- ◆ Make it your mission to show up and love kids every day and you won't go wrong!

References

Griffith, O. M. (2014). Gratitude: A powerful tool for your classroom. *Edutopia.org*. www.edutopia.org/blog/gratitude-powerful-tool-for-classroom-owen-griffith.

Hughes, R., Kinder A., & Cooper, C. (2019). *The Wellbeing Workout*. Cham: Palgrave Macmillan. https://doi-org.ezproxy.bethel.edu/10.1007/978-3-319-92552-3_60.

Joseph, S., & Wood, A. (2010). Assessment of positive functioning in clinical psychology: Theoretical and practical issues. *Clinical Psychology Review*, vol. 30, no. 7, pp. 830–38.

Ruini, C. (2017). *Positive Psychology in the Clinical Domains: Research and Practice*. Cham: Springer International Publishing. https://doi.org/10.1007/978-3-319-52112-1.

Shapiro, F. R. (2014). Who wrote the serenity prayer? *The Chronicle of Higher Education*, vol. 60, no. 33, Chronicle of Higher Education, Inc.

Toepfer, S. M., Cichy, K., & Peters, P. (2012). Letters of gratitude: Further evidence for author benefits. *Journal of Happiness Studies*, vol. 13, no. 1, pp. 187–201.

Watkins, P. C., Uhder, J., & Pichinevskiy, S. (2014). Grateful recounting enhances subjective well-being: The importance of grateful processing. *The Journal of Positive Psychology*, pp. 1–8, doi:10.1080/17439760.2014.927909.

Wehmeyer, M. L. (2013). *The Oxford Handbook of Positive Psychology and Disability*. Oxford, UK: Oxford University Press.

Wood, A. M., Joseph, S., & Maltby, J. (2009). Gratitude predicts psychological wellbeing above the big five facets. *Personality and Individual Differences*, vol. 46, no. 4, pp. 443–7, doi:10.1016/j.paid.2008.11.012.

Made in the USA
Monee, IL
12 January 2023

25163246R00120